THE BODY OF A FROG

A MEMOIR ON SELF-LOATHING, SELF-LOVE, AND TRANSGENDER PREGNANCY

AARRON SHOLAR

atmosphere press

Published by Atmosphere Press

Cover design by Felipe Betim

Atmospherepress.com

PRAISE FOR **THE BODY OF A FROG**

"In this world often resistant to change, Aarron Sholar has written a memoir that shows readers the difficult yet rewarding journey one experiences when embracing authenticity. Sholar tells us his story of transformation with candor and honesty. Through this book, readers will broaden their perspectives and knowledge about gender identity and the importance of staying true to oneself. While reading this book, I felt like I was listening to a good friend. Sholar uses the guiding image of the mutable rain frog to help us see that even when faced with challenges, we can adapt, change and find a way to survive."

–Rachael Hanel, professor of creative nonfiction at Minnesota State University, Mankato, & author of *We'll Be the Last Ones to Let You Down: Memoir of a Gravedigger's Daughter*

"Heart-wrenching but ultimately redemptive, *The Body of a Frog* charts Aarron Sholar's journey from self-harm to self-love, eloquently tracing the joys and sorrows of one man's dysmorphic odyssey to redefine masculinity. Raw, lyrical, and courageous, Sholar's memoir should be required reading for all who struggle to accept themselves and their bodies, as well as for those seeking to understand the personal struggles—and triumphs—of the transgender experience. A triumph."

–Matthew Vollmer, author of *All of Us Together in the End*

For AJ, who taught me that I deserve to be loved.

CONTENTS

IV

V

In 2006, the mutable rainfrog was discovered as the first vertebrate that can change its skin texture. When threatened, the frog will go from a smooth, what-one-would-expect skin texture to a spiky one. Once the threat is gone, the texture will return to that of a typical, normal frog.[1]

---

[1] Oskin, Becky. Shape-Shifting Frog Can Change Its Skin Texture. (2015). livescience

A HATRED IS BORN

I sat on the carpeted floor of my third-grade classroom, my feet flat and my knees arched before me in the air. My flowy, nature-green skirt with white flowers on it exposed the shorts I was wearing under it (I never sat "properly" in it, so they were a precaution). We were supposed to be watching a video about how bread is made in factories, but my attention was drawn away and to my calf. I swayed my leg back and forth, watching the fat, what I called the *squish* at the time, follow. I reached out, gripping it in my hand, watching the skin and fat pour out between my fingers. I sat crisscross, and the squish, well, *squished* up against my thigh; I slid my legs flat, and the squish leaked out the sides and looked like a pancake on the floor—there was no escape, no mistaking that this was my body. On this day, I decided I hated my body.

"Ninety-seven percent of women say they have at least one negative thought about their body image every single day."[1]

I imagine all women have a time like this, one where they can pinpoint exactly when they started to hate their bodies. I wonder how naturally this comes to us, if it is just an inherent part of life, or if something tells us to hate ourselves. No

---

[1] Survey: 97 percent of women have negative body image. (March 2, 2011). CBS News.

one ever told me that my legs were too fat or too jiggly; I just looked at them and decided that for myself. When I was growing up, all my classmates seemingly had no issues with their bodies—they could wear all the skirts and booty shorts they wanted, while I couldn't even manage to don a shirt with a neckline any lower than a standard men's T-shirt.

THE PROBLEM WITH BREASTS

My breasts became a problem near the end of fourth grade, only a year after I'd discovered my squish. My sister and I would stand on our mom's and dad's bed, convinced it was a wrestling ring. The bed frame was that natural, yellow teak color that so much wood furniture was in the early to mid-2000s, and four wooden, decorative poles erupted from each corner, nearly poking the smooth ceiling. They were already a tad worn from our prior use. On this particular day, we decided to be sumo wrestlers.

We spread our legs as far apart as we could, bending our knees at 90-degree angles. I pulled my shirt off, and my mom wandered in moments later. I imagine she froze for only a moment before grabbing my arm, pulling me off her bed, into my room, and throwing my shirt at me.

Put your shirt back on!

My child mind was very confused. I could take my shirt off before, and in my own opinion, the just-barely-pubescent breasts made the sumo fight more realistic. I shuffled my shirt on and sat there momentarily—why can't I take my shirt off now? My older brother and younger sister could. The idea of breasts being "bad" or "sexual" hadn't occurred to me yet. Heck, the idea of a body being something to hide hadn't even crossed my mind; I bathed with my sister, and my friends and I changed in the same room before going to the pool, so since when did I have to hide?

When my mom dragged my shirtless self to my room and threw my shirt at me, I became aware of my body in a way I hadn't known was possible. This body was something to hide from the world, suddenly gross. I refused to wear bras for at least a year after that day. I came out from the shower one day, the towel wrapped around my barely pubescent breasts. I wandered into my room to grab some fresh clothes and was shocked to find some sort of odd-looking clothing in the drawer. The thing was a small, rectangular piece of cloth. It was white with green trim and straps and had multi-colored polka dots on it. There were no "humps" for more developed breasts to sit in it like in the ones I'd see at Target. *Where does this go?* The only underwear I'd known was the kind that goes around your waist. I slowly pulled it from the drawer, laying it on the carpet before my knees. I stared it down, trying not to touch it much.

A few days later, my young self approached Mom, starter bra in hand. I brought it to my hips and looked at her: *How do I wear this?* She took it from me and held it to my chest: *It goes up here.*

I still refused it. It was constricting my chest; the straps were uncomfortable, and I was just a stubborn pre-teen. My best friend, Katie, wore undershirts often since she was small-chested and could get away with it. So, I took after her and wore undershirts, too. *I just have to wear something under my shirt, so I'll wear these instead,* I told myself. My mom didn't like my idea, though.

We were walking into church; I was wearing my new favorite shirt, which was cream-colored with a cute brown puppy and a bowtie on the front. Now, my mom had told me several times that I needed to wear a bra under it because of the see-through color, but as kids often do, I refused to listen, as I had worn it to church without anything under it before with no problem. Right before stepping into the building, Mom gripped my arm and pulled me aside. I watched the rest of the family continue as if they were oblivious that we'd stopped.

You can't go in there like that.

Why? I like this shirt—

I told you, you have to wear at least SOMETHING under it.

Why though? I've never worn anything under it before—

Well, now you have to.

My mom turned and walked away from me, following the rest of the family into the building. I hesitated for a moment as I watched her walk off. I was alone because my body was developing in ways I didn't want it to. I didn't want these breasts; I wanted to be free. That shirt wasn't my favorite anymore. Mom and I compromised, and I was allowed to wear my treasured undershirt at church for a few weeks, but it was uncomfortable there. The double layers made me feel thick, large, just not like myself. I stopped wearing the dog shirt.

What was a ten-year-old supposed to make of this? I wore those rectangular cloths, the training bras, from then on, but my mind was busy worrying about building a new Thomas the Tank Engine set in the basement, not if I was wearing a bra or not. Frankly, I didn't care about those bras.

THE PERIOD CURSE

I encountered the next worst step in puberty, the period, days before my tenth birthday. The plan was to go to Shadow Land, the local laser tag arena, to play a few games with my friends and siblings. But my body had other ideas.

I sat on the toilet at home; the bowl filled with a mixture of water and blood. Bile threatened to erupt from my throat as I felt the thick, clumped blood drip from inside my body into the water. I couldn't stand from where I was, and I felt that I couldn't call out for my mom to help. I felt embarrassed.

Months earlier, at my pediatrician's suggestion, mom brought a different type of book to my room to read before bed. We'd usually read Narnia (my favorite series because of her) or Roald Dahl books, but she appeared in the doorway holding a pink-and-yellow book. There might have been a picture of a barely pubescent girl on the front. Inside were paragraphs about how I'll begin to bleed intensely every month for the next 40 to 50 years, diagrams of my private parts, etc. I was straight-up confused. My mom was explaining menstruation and how you bleed from a hole, but my young mind couldn't make the connection between having a hole down there and blood coming from it, so I asked: *Does a hole just open like on my side, bleed for a week, and then close itself back up? Like a weird wound?* She reassured me that I already had this hole and always will. This hole would become something to avoid in the coming years.

But even as I barely lifted my butt off the toilet seat to reach into the cabinet across the bathroom to grab the pads my mom had told me probably just days prior, it didn't click. It was me and my body, forced against each other, like Romeo and Juliet. I didn't want Her—my female anatomy, my vagina. An urge inside me told me to hate it, not to touch it.

I ripped the flimsy yet obnoxiously loud packaging open, pulled it from the sticky side of the pad, and then stopped. Mom never showed me how to put this thing on, and now that I was confronted with my own body. I had to figure out how to use it as soon as possible. I guess my young mind didn't think to put the softer side facing upwards, so I stuck the thing onto the bottom of my underwear so that the part that absorbs everything was facing down.

This style of pad was not helpful in the slightest.

I wore this ineffective item throughout all of laser tag. *This isn't so bad*, I thought at first, but once my mom found out and I told her how I'd put the pad on, she corrected my strategy, and for some reason, the actual way to put one on was much more uncomfortable.

My cousin told me that your period starts when you're around thirteen, but I misheard her, that it *stops* when you're thirteen. I was ten at the time, and so I was absolutely ecstatic when I heard that it'd only be a few years of this bloody hell. I ran downstairs to tell my mom; I can't remember if she choked or chuckled a little. *No, hun, it STARTS when you're thirteen for most girls, but it goes on until you're near sixty.*

In her graphic memoir, *Fun Home*, Alison Bechdel describes her own experience in getting her period. She explains that in her diary, which she wrote in every day, she avoided even writing the words "menstruation" or "period;" instead, she opted to represent those weeks with a simple "x." When the blood appears for the first time, she brushes it off, but once it comes back, she deduces that maybe this is something she should mention to her mom. By the time she mentions it to her mom, she writes that she didn't even document this in her beloved diary. And she wrote everything in that diary. The period was ignored, or, more likely, it was avoided.[1]

In 2017, Columbia University reported that girls across America feel unprepared for puberty, especially those from low-income households. Specifically, the girls surveyed "feel they lack the information and readiness to cope with the onset of menstruation."[2] With the age of puberty in girls steadily lowering, and with some girls getting their first periods at eight years old, the need for readiness is ever important. Dr. Marni Sommer tells readers that "'the transition through puberty is a critical period of development that provides an important opportunity to build a healthy foundation for sexual and reproductive health.' "[3] I understand this entirely. I wasn't ready for puberty when I opened my first pad before laser tag; I wasn't ready for puberty when I couldn't wear that dog shirt anymore. I wasn't ready for anything, even after my mom read that book to me and explained the pictures inside it. When it came to my own body, I wasn't ready for it to change in those ways I despised. I wanted to change it on my own accord, not whatever that was.

Melissa Febos, author of *Body Work*, *Abandon Me: Memoirs*, and other works, developed breasts earlier than her peers. Her

---

[1] "Bechdel, Alison. *Fun Home*. (2006). Mariner Books

[2] Study Finds Girls Feel Unprepared for Puberty. (2017). publichealth.columbia.edu

[3] Ibid

own and others' reactions to them were anything but positive: "Until age 11, I was a confident, athletic child. Tanned and strong, I played barefoot all summer in our rural New England neighborhood and took pride in the bruises and scrapes that mapped the days across my limbs. Then, my breasts arrived: huge, heavy and first among my peers. They marked the before and after of my body—what it meant in the world of people and what it meant to me."[4] Before, my body was a body that was the same as everyone else's. But now, it was overrun with breasts, blood, and things unwanted. If only they could actually be desired. But what would that take? I could never imagine myself wanting to get my period.

The most devastating thing about this period was that when it came each month, I couldn't even go to the pool. When I was in middle school, I went to a week-long sleep-over Bible camp for a week; the camp itself was actually really fun, located on the Jersey Shore with beaches in any direction. The first days of camp had their routines: get there, bring our things to our shared rooms, and then, as a group, go take the swimming test, which you had to pass in order to swim, so we all just got it out of the way immediately. One year, I think my seventh-grade year, we were in our shared room, all getting into our swimsuits. I meandered towards our counselor and, keeping my voice as quiet as possible, explained:

I can't take the swim test; I got my puberty thing—
Your what?
You know, the monthly thing.
Oh! You're on your period! I have some tampons if you want one. Do you know how to use them?
No ...

---

[4] Febos, Melissa. The feminist case for breast reduction. (May 11, 2022). *NYTimes*

Oh. Well, that's okay! I'll just tell the lifeguard that you'll take it later on this week.

Okay, please don't tell the lifeguard that I'm on it, please?

She nodded in agreement.

When the time came for all of us to go swim, I joined the crowd, but I was the only kid, girl or boy, who was still in their regular clothes. Everyone lined up at the edge of the pool, the first kids jumping in. All we had to do was swim to the other end of the pool. One after the other, everyone jumped in and took off. Once they were halfway down the pool, there went the next person. I stood and watched—and stayed quiet when they asked me why I wasn't swimming. *She's going to come back and do it later,* was all our leader told them. But in my mind, I was sure that everyone knew I was on my period. I knew, so everyone else had to, too.

I was worried everyone would know that my body was bleeding and that they'd know that was gross, just as I thought. I remembered moments in school when the boys would tease girls about periods. One time, a classmate got up to use the bathroom, and a group of boys asked her from across the room, *Ooooo, did you get your period?* Followed by some chuckles. I didn't want to get chuckled at like her.

On the weeks I'd get my period, it was guaranteed that I'd wake up at least once overnight to change my pad. One night, I woke up, climbed out of my top bunk, and meandered towards the bathroom. I gagged through the whole process, still not accustomed to the sight, the smell, and even the concept that I'd have to live with this for most of my life. But once it was done, I wandered back to the bedroom I shared with my sister. I tossed the used pad in the small trash can, climbed up my ladder, and burrito-d back into my covers. The next day, I woke up to my little sister, who hadn't experienced puberty yet, standing by the trash can, looking at the wrapped-up pad inside.

You're not a baby; why do you have to wear diapers?

I paused. My mom had told me once I started my period that if my sister asked about it, I shouldn't tell her anything, that I ignore her or brush it off. My mom wanted to take that responsibility upon herself, to teach her when it was necessary for her.

It's not a diaper.

Then what is it?

It's nothing.

I imagine my sister grilled me for answers after that, trying to get me to crack. But as my mom and the rest of society had taught me, my body was not for anyone else, so I held strong and let her think I had to wear diapers as a pre-teen.

Rachel Hatzipanagos, a blogger, has similar feelings around periods specifically: "I don't know where I learned to be ashamed. I just knew, like how we know what hunger is before we learn the word to describe it."[5]

According to historian Lara Freidenfelds, "how American women manage and approach menstruation is called the 'modern period' ... It's the idea that your body does not undermine your ability to be productive at school or at work," Freidenfelds said in an interview; "it's a body that doesn't smell or have cramps."[6]

[5.] Hatzipanagos, Rachel. Why we're taught to hide our periods. (2017). thelily.com

[6.] Ibid

Screw the "modern period;" I wanted the "no period." I didn't want the cramps, the blood, the breasts—I didn't want this female body.

GOD TELLS ME TO HATE MY BODY

I wonder how we learn to hate a body. Is it like writing, where if you are with it enough, you can see flaws in it that others may not? Or maybe we're taught—being in society for even one day will show you how women are taught to hate their bodies, even at ages as young as two or three. When childhood beauty pageant contestants were surveyed, the research found "a significant association between childhood beauty pageant participation and increased body dissatisfaction," that "females who had participated in beauty pageants perceived their current figure as larger, and preferred their figure to be smaller... depression scores were higher, and self-esteem scores lower, for those who had participated in beauty pageants compared to those who had not."[1]

Or maybe the hatred of my body can be of religious origins—growing up, I learned from our Evangelical church that bodies aren't to be offered to others. It was the usual "your body is a temple" one month of every year at Sunday school. During this month, the boys and girls were divided up and taught in separate rooms about purity, what the Bible says about sex,

---

[1] Wonderlich, Anna L., Ackard, Diann M., Henderson, Judith B. Childhood Beauty Pageant Contestants: Associations with Adult Disordered Eating and Mental Health. (2007). *The Journal of Treatment and Prevention*, 13(3), 291-301.

etc. The girls were taught at one end of the building, and the boys were taught at the opposite end.

One year, the format was different: the boys and girls were together for two weeks and then separated the last two. These first two weeks, we learned about the tale of Sodom and Gomorrah—the classic adultery Bible story.

The story goes like this (Genesis 19:4-7,11,14-17):

4 the men of the city, even the men of Sodom, compassed the house round, both old and young, all the people from every quarter.

5 And they called unto Lot, and said unto him, Where are the men which came into thee this night? bring them unto us, that we may know them.

6 And Lot went out at the door unto them, and shut the door after him,

7 And said, I pray you, brethren, do not so wickedly.

11 And they smote the men that were at the door of the house with blindness, both small and great: so that they wearied themselves to find the door.

14 And Lot went out, and spake unto his sons in law, which married his daughters, and said, Up, get you out of this place; for the LORD will destroy this city. But he seemed as one that mocked unto his sons in law.

15 And when the morning arose, then the angels hastened Lot, saying, Arise, take thy wife, and thy two daughters, which are here; lest thou be consumed in the iniquity of the city.

16 And while he lingered, the men laid hold upon his hand, and upon the hand of his wife, and upon the hand of his two daughters; the LORD being merciful unto him: and they brought him forth, and set him without the city.

17 And it came to pass, when they had brought them forth abroad, that he said, Escape for thy life; look not behind thee, neither stay thou in all the plain; escape to the mountain, lest thou be consumed.[2]

For those of you who didn't have this story drilled in your head as a teenager at church, Sodom was a city that became very well-known for its raunchy citizens, who often engaged in highly sexual acts and were looked down upon by God. The men who were banging on Lot's door were doing this because they wanted to have sex with his virgin daughter. Since this city was so sinful, God planned to destroy it with fire. Lot knew this, and so he took his daughter and wife to escape. As they were escaping, his wife looked back at the city, which God said specifically not to do. And so, when she looked, she was turned into a pillar of salt. My church took this story and taught us that God doesn't like when we sin, even more so if it is in a sexual manner. My middle-school self was determined to not turn into a pillar of salt.

I wonder if that church is the reason why I couldn't bring myself to show any cleavage or my thighs for the longest time, why even today when I see women walking across the university campus in shorts that I'd say barely comply as shorts, I worry for them. I hid my body from the world, even from myself. In sixth grade, my sister and I got separate rooms as we were getting older, and keeping two teenage girls in the same small bedroom is not a good idea for most parents. So, I got my own room, and my mom and I went to IKEA to pick out some bedspreads, maybe a lamp, and a mirror. I looked at the mirrors, watching my reflection walk from one to the other.

---

[2] Sodom and Gomorrah. kingjamesbibleonline.com

My mom brought me to one that showed my head, shoulders, and entire torso. She stood behind me, her hands on my arms.

What do you think about this one?

The mirror was a variation of a square. There was a square in the middle, lined with straight cuts in the glass. There were smaller squares at each corner of the middle one, so it looked like it had little ears and feet. Arched rectangles connected the smaller squares. All in all, it was a chunky square. When I stood in front of it, I asked my mom:

Why do I need one in my room? Can't I use the mirror in the bathroom?

Everyone needs a mirror in their room—what if you wanna do your hair or try on an outfit?

Fine, I'll get this one. I pointed to the square-ish one in front of me.

I didn't do my hair in that mirror, nor did I try on my outfits. I knew how I looked in my comfort clothes of baggy pants and a T-shirt a size or two too large.

A short time after we got the mirror hung up, I considered covering it with newspaper like the teenage girls in those early 2000s movies would do with pictures of cute boys. But I wanted to cover mine entirely. I wanted to hide my body from myself.

My church told me that my body wasn't for anyone besides myself, and I told myself that it wasn't for me, either. I felt that in order to be accepted, to be a good young woman, I had to be pure.

A guest contributor on the website *Desiring God* blogs about purity:

"Sex has become a 'right' and a means of expressing personal 'identity.' People 'hook up' without any intention of a deep relationship. And far more sinister, we see consequences of this moral shift in the deaths of millions of children who, through no choice of their own, are sacrificed on the altar of our sexual freedom ... Sex is not a right, nor did God design it to define our 'identity.' Our identity is in being children of God. It is not meant to be a way to gain power or acceptance. Men and women of God do not use sex as a means of gratifying selfish desires, but instead, lovingly as a means of serving one another in genuine intimacy and love in marriage. Valuing and pursuing purity will honor God and heighten the joy we experience in this wonderful gift."[3]

On the other end of the argument, the website *Women and the Church* says this on purity:

"Women often learn to hate their bodies early on. The moment they have their first mense, if not earlier, is the moment they become responsible for everyone around them. At the same time, they are also denying that they feel anything at all. This culture is reinforced by adults and other believers. Being perceived as anything less than pure, often means being shunned and made fun of by others in the church or Christian culture."[4]

My middle school self was just a body. I was not to wear tank tops, booty shorts, low-cut shirts, short skirts, tight clothing, etc. What would happen if I wore these types of clothing? Men would lust after me, which, of course, would always be my fault. For one month straight, every year, I'd hear how us girls don't want the boys to stare at us out of sin. We don't

---

[3] Adrien, Segal. What I Wish I Had Known About Purity. (2018). *Desiring God*

[4] Purity Culture. womenandchurch.org

want to make boys sin, as if we have any control over what boys would say or do.

One day, I bought a shirt that was a bit more fitting than the T-shirts I rocked every day. The shirt hugged my stomach that I thought was too large, it hugged my breasts that I strived to hide, and it was white, so any bra or even undershirt I would wear under it was visible to everyone. I'd see the other girls in school wear white shirts without a problem, but I've never quite figured out how they managed. My body was not for others; it was barely for me.

I felt like I was just a body. And not even a body I liked.

ONCE A BODY,
ALWAYS A BODY

Just a body. What does it mean to be just a body?

I was a body when I was adopted, too. My parents adopted me internationally, them in America and my fresh-baby-self in Russia—Novosibirsk, to be exact. Before my parents actually traveled to meet and adopt me, they were sent a VHS tape. The tape was nothing special, just some sweet Russian women recording me doing baby things. My adoptive parents saw me eating food, with the Russian women saying only one thing understandable in English: *This is Tatiana Reyabova.* Then I was on a sort of changing table, naked for all the eyes to see, complete with a blue X on one butt cheek to indicate which one I'd gotten my shots on. Then, I was in a playpen with some other kids. A Russian woman handed me a sort of rattle and put a hard plastic bunny in front of me. I looked directly at the camera and started to hit the bunny with the rattle. Then, I was on the floor, standing and wandering with another set of kids. I'm handed a green, also hard plastic, dinosaur toy, but I just throw it on the floor. I'm handed it again, and again it's thrown on the floor. My parents saw this and somehow decided I was the one. But they didn't know anything about me; I was just this orphaned child, my birth mother having abandoned me at the hospital. I was just a body on a square TV screen, yet I meant so much to them already.

If I can mean so much to them, I can mean a lot to other people, too, right?

I think about the children who do not get adopted. Just like in America, the older the kid, the less likely they are to get adopted. What makes it worse is that "in reality, there are almost no orphans as such in the country. At least 80 percent of the so-called orphans have at least one living parent. Their parents have abandoned them or been deprived of parental rights because of parental alcoholism, drug use or child abuse," *The Moscow Times* reports.[1] Once they're out of the orphanage, their only option, realistically, is to join the military. That's all life holds for these orphans—they're just a body for the country that abandoned them.

I imagine my parents thought I was just the cutest kid when they saw that video, clad in a deep-blue dress with a matching bow on top of my head, one that was just about as big as my face. Maybe I was the perfect kid in their eyes, a child they'd been waiting for and finally found. Me, my body, was once so valued; I wonder how I went from this amazing, blue-dressed child to the third-grader who realized that her body was not one she ever thought she could love. I became this child who hated her body—how it was, how it changed, and what it would become. When I first noticed hair under my arms, I was wearing a pair of light blue jean shorts with a little tank top that was a mustard yellow with sunflowers all over it. I liked it because it had a bra built in, so I didn't have to wear

---

[1] Phillips, Alan. Russia's Orphanages: A Leftover From Soviet Past. (March 18, 2013). *The Moscow Times*

anything else with it. I sat at my desk and slipped my hands into my armpits for whatever reason, but something wasn't right. The skin was rough, like little goosebumps were all over it. I was used to this skin feeling smooth and naked. I felt the other side; the bumps were there too. I didn't want to look at the areas—I was scared of what I would find. For the rest of the school day, I'd slip a hand under, feel the bumps, let worry fill me up, and return my hands to doing my schoolwork. I got home and didn't mention it to my mom, and she never really mentioned it to me. In the mirror, I saw the gnarly, unruly even, hair living in my armpits. *I can't wear my sunflowers anymore*, I told myself. Bummer, that one was my favorite shirt.

I wanted, no, I *needed* to regain control of my body. I didn't want to be the girl who squeezed her legs every time she sat down, just watching the skin seemingly pour out all over. Gaining control of our bodies, maintaining bodily autonomy, is a hill that this girl did not want to climb.

And so, she didn't.

She didn't but *he* did.

The frog has to change, or else it risks being eaten. I had to change, or else I risked being eaten—by the world, this thing we live called life. Life threatened me with depression after handling a body I hated. If I hadn't changed, where would I be now? All I can say is that my ghost would be hanging out around some train tracks beneath a bridge.

MY BODY AS FEMININE

In sixth grade, I wandered down into the basement and dug in the plastic tub that held nerf guns, toys that hadn't seen the light of day for years, and little bouncy balls, like the ones you'd get from the machines at Old Navy. I pulled out some bouncy balls. I felt each ball's texture, rubbing my thumb across them. There was a yellow tie-dye one that was shiny but also had a very plastic-rubbery texture. My thumbs, sweating just a little from this act I knew I was not supposed to be doing, made a *squeeeeak* on the surface. I threw it back into the bin. I picked one up that was a purple-y, pink-y color. This one was the same size (it could easily fit in my palm), and the texture was different. It was softer. It was plastic, but it's almost like no waxy finish was added to it. Perfect.

I took the little ball into my dad's bathroom, the only one in the basement, and cleaned it thoroughly—the smell is still so distinct to me. I can't quite explain it. Just wash rubber with soap and water, you'll know what I mean—pulled down my pants, set the ball in the trough of the underwear, right where my pad would normally go, and pulled everything back up. I arranged the ball so that there was just the slightest bulge in my pants underneath my basketball shorts. I turned to the side to admire it. I wore the ball around the house, rearranging it to snap a picture with my brick of an LG Cosmos phone— the one with the sliding keyboard, now *those* were revolutionary. But I'd erase the picture right away. Then I'd take the ball out and throw it in the garbage. *I'm not supposed to be doing this; this isn't what girls do. I'm not a boy.* I repeated this process until there were no bouncy balls left in that tub.

Other attempts were simpler—as a pre-teen, I got a majority of my clothes from Justice. The smaller clothing items, like panties, shorts, bras, etc., were arranged on these circular tables that looked more like they were meant to have Asian cuisine eaten off them. I wandered to one with what I called "booty shorts" on them. Realistically, they showed no booty; they came down maybe an inch or two below the butt—but they were shorter than what I was used to. This pair was a basic orange with white stitching. I looked at the shorts, hesitant, but I felt like there were voices in my head all telling me how pretty I could look in them. I got home and slid the orange shorts on—I couldn't bring myself to wear them. I felt exposed, naked, just not myself. My Aunt Jean said they looked nice on me, but they sat in my dresser drawer until we decided to donate them to the church's Free Flea.

"By the time I was 12, my body felt like a disguise that I couldn't take off," Febos says.[1]

My body, too, was a disguise that I wanted to succumb to—but could not. No amount of clothing could convince me that this was how my body was supposed to be. *I must have to make my body myself*, I decided.

Those orange shorts represented femininity, something I not only avoided but completely rejected in my teenage years. If I wore shorts like all the other girls at school, I'd have to

---

[1] Febos, Melissa. The feminist case for breast reduction. (May 11, 2022). *NYTimes*

shave more leg hair, and I'd worry about the tightness show-ing everyone when I was on my period, the outline of the pad making it clear. I'd feel uncomfortable. I once let my sister put nail polish on me, but that one time was more than enough. I know for kids growing up today, things like make-up, nail pol-ish, pink, traditionally "boy" or "girl" things are embraced as being for all children, but even as recently as the early 2000s, this was not as much the case. I was still raised with the men-tality, be it purposeful, which I don't think was the case, or an effect of society's subliminal messaging, that boys do boy things and girls do girl things. When my sister put nail polish on me that day, my fingers felt heavy. My mom showed me how to get it off with the remover, which reeked of chemi-cals and slight lemon. Heck, my child mind denoted non-fem-inine things as feminine somehow, too—it took me until high school to finally let mom smack some Aquaphor on my hands; only a year or two ago, I started using ChapStick religiously, as for most of my life, I had equated it to lipstick.

It was in 1924 that Freud decided that anatomy and biology were the key determiners of our gender. TIME claims that "critics have been objecting to body parts as central predictors of one's professional and personal path" since then.[2] *Teaching LGBTQ History* provides a slideshow of how gender roles and norms in the US have changed over time:

> In the Victorian Era: Rigid gender roles, "Women were thought to be kind, tender, emotional, and domestic. They were expected to cook, clean, and take care of the children. Men were thought to be strong, logical, tough, and aggressive. They were expected to participate in politics and make money."

---

2. Weingarten, Elizabeth. How To Shake Up Gender Norms. (January 20, 2015). *TIME*

In the Second Industrial Revolution (Late 1800s - Early 1900s): "Women, especially poor women, were sought after by factory employees, as they generally had smaller hands which was good for machine work. Employers could also pay women and children less than adult men. Women became very active in factory work, especially in the Northeast's textile mills."

In the Early 1900s: the beginning of Feminism, women began to do "men's work" and began to fight for equal political rights. White women are given the right to vote via the 19th Amendment. "Flapper" fashions had women expressing themselves more sexually.

During WWII: Women became primary manufacturers for the war. Rosie the Riveter becomes an icon.

In the 1960s: Women had access to birth control, could go to Ivy League Schools, and more. Equal pay began to be a hot topic in debates.[3]

As society continues to evolve and grow, it's almost as if men's and women's roles intertwine, blurring the lines between what to associate with men and what to associate with women. Women started out with absolutely no autonomy over themselves, their abilities, and their bodies. By now, the degree of women's autonomy is significantly more, but still fluctuating, especially with the overturning of Roe v. Wade. In 2023, language around gender is blurring. More and more people are saying that men can have babies, that the term "mother" is inconsiderate and discriminatory. But it's not men who can have babies; it's transsexual men—those born female who suffer from gender dysphoria. But does that mean men *can* have babies? Could *I* have a baby? Sure, I could, if I wanted to, I suppose.

---

[3] Solberg, Carly, and Klein, Matthew. Shifting Gender Roles in the US. lgbtqhistory.com

Who gives anyone bodily autonomy? Does it come with our first breath of life? Does it come with our first words? Can it be taken? Can it be given back? Can it be gained by changing our bodies?

My mom taught me how to shave in eighth grade. She handed me a razor and told me the two basic steps:

1. Put soap all over your leg, and

2. Shave in the opposite direction that the hair falls.

I wandered into the shower and spent the next 30 minutes doing just that. I felt my leg afterward, amazed that this soft skin was hidden beneath the seemingly unruly leg hair that had grown a year or two ago. I continued this routine every week; I could not have any leg hair showing because the other girls at school didn't have any, and neither did my own mom.

With puberty came pubic hair, which was even thicker than my leg hair. When I'd have to change pads at school, I made sure to grip the hair tightly and slide the piece of toilet paper downward so I got the blood clumps out entirely. My privates began to disappear in the forest until I couldn't see what was down there anymore.

My sister had a friend over one day—I was on my top bunk of the cream-white bunkbed, and she and the friend were playing with toys on the floor. For some reason, as I was trying to leave my spot, they ventured up the ladder and blocked my exit path. My sister held me down on the bed, and her friend gripped my shorts, yanking them down, along with the fitted underwear. Everything was unveiled as her friend's eyes widened at the sight: so much dark hair that everything else was encased in it. After that moment, I remember nothing.

When did I lose my bodily autonomy? Maybe it was after that moment that I noticed the hair that ran all over my legs, or maybe it was when I first felt my armpit hair, which was just as thick as the rest of the hair, and my mom told me I had to shave it because *girls don't have armpit hair.*

In 2010, my Aunt Ruthie posted a picture on Facebook of me, my cousin, and my younger sister at the pool. My sister stands to the far right, her bright blonde shoulder-length hair contrasting the top of her one-piece suit. The bottom half was bright pink with typical white flowers on it. My cousin has frizzy brown hair that is slightly longer than my sister's. She wears a turquoise bikini that shows the most skin out of all three of us. Then there's me, not even in a traditional women's bathing suit. I wore a pink rash guard with flowers, still girly enough, and a pair of pink swim trunks that came down to the middle of my thigh. My shoulders were slumped forward a tad, and my obscene straight-across-my-forehead bangs tried to cover my eyes. I used that outfit to hide, to obscure my body—not only was the body hair a thing to hide, but most of my body had to hide, too.

When I felt this urge to hide as much of my body as possible, *that's* when I lost my bodily autonomy.

HOW TO MODIFY A BODY

I feel differently than but similar to Febos. We both changed our bodies after experiencing female puberty, and we both struggled with this puberty. This struggle, she explains, is due to the fact that her "perception of [herself] could never be entirely sealed off from other people's perceptions."[1]

People make themselves individuals, *themselves*, through clothing, haircuts and colors, what they do in their free time, and, for many young adults, through body modification.

1,901,049 people sought and received cosmetic surgery in 2000. This number would increase by 22% by 2020, bringing the number of people getting cosmetic surgery to 2,314,720 a mere twenty years later. 92% of these people getting surgery are female.[2]

Since 2013, studies have seen an increase in people under 30 seeking plastic surgery: "those roughly between 23 and 38 years old—have increased the demand for plastic-surgery procedures because of their fixation with self-care." Many "millennials

---

[1] Febos, Melissa. The feminist case for breast reduction. (May 11, 2022). *NYTimes*

[2] Ali, Rasha. Selfies and self-care are leading millennials to get more cosmetic procedures, study says. (January 24, 2019). *USA Today*

[also] aren't necessarily getting drastic cosmetic surgeries; they're more focused on remaining youthful and looking as natural as possible—because of that self-care piece."[3]

Change is becoming self-care, not something that's necessary due to others' perceptions of us.

Other people go to more out-there measures to get a body they're happy with. Michael Jackson claimed he only ever had his nose done to help his breathing and singing abilities, but surgeons and researchers have decided that the total number of surgeries the King of Pop had was over 100.[4] Though we can't know his intentions, from an outsider's perspective and mine, it seems that the star was never really content with the way his face looked. If he was still alive, I can't help but wonder what his face would look like now—even more unrecognizable?

Rajee Narinesingh is a trans woman who attended a "pumping party" in 2005—a party where women would go to a "doctor's" house to get injections in their faces, buttocks; you name it, it was "pumped." Many of these alleged "doctors" actually were not doctors, and better yet, they were using items that you should *never* inject into anyone, such as "super glue, mineral oil and tire sealant." What did the "doctor" whom Narinesingh visited use? Cement. This woman lived with cement in her cheeks, face, and chin for years until surgeons were able to successfully and safely remove it all. Her reason for doing this? She claimed that "the last thing I wanted was

---

3. Ibid

4. White, Tiffany. How Much Plastic Surgery Did Michael Jackson Have Done? Watch His Face Transform Over Time. (2018). *Life & Style*

to look like a man in a dress … I wanted to be a beautiful woman."[5]

Maybe the desire for bodily autonomy is just called being human. Why else would Michael Jackson rearrange his face so often? Or Narinesingh get cement injected into her face? Or I ruin all the house's perfectly good bouncy balls?

Why else would I dig into my skin with
toothpicks every night?

---

[5] Buchanan, Sarah. Trans woman who injected cement into face is unrecognisable after life-changing surgery. (May 12, 2016). *Daily Star*

HOW TO ~~MODIFY~~ MUTILATE A BODY

Toothpicks were not as painful as real knives or razors; I wanted to hurt myself without risking severe injury or death. There was one time when my mom did see those fresh cuts on my skin, too—

It was Christmas, normally a time of joy and happiness. When my uncle and aunt come to the house, since my bedroom is technically the guest bedroom as well, I'd spend a week or so on the top bunk of my sister's bed. One Christmas Eve, my mom was saying her usual goodnights. She stood on the wicker basket by the side of the bed to hoist herself up so she could say goodnight to me. That's when she noticed the cuts. I'm not sure if she accidentally saw them or if I just didn't care if she saw them. She examined them:

What happened?

Cat got them.

Hold on—

She went into her bathroom and came back with a hefty squeeze tube of Neosporin. She rubbed it over the cuts and kissed me goodnight. When she left, I immediately rubbed the cream off onto the bed sheets. I couldn't let her ruin my only source of the control that I wanted over this changing body.

Leah J. Orchinik from Nemours Children's Health explains that "some people [harm themselves] because they feel desperate for relief from bad feelings. People may not know better ways to get relief from emotional pain or pressure. For some, it's an expression of strong feelings like rage, sorrow, rejection, desperation, longing, or emptiness."[1]

I can't say why I wanted to hurt myself back then, why every time a cut was just on the verge of healing itself, I'd open it up again. I ask myself, *Why did you do that? This body did nothing to you.* But it did—it changed in those ways I didn't warrant. Those ways I didn't want one bit. It's other people who took this body from you. No one, others or myself, approves of this body. I couldn't live with that body.

Maybe we need to hurt, injure, mutilate, and put our bodies through hell to really appreciate them.

"I was sure it [For Febos: breast reduction; for me: a double mastectomy] would have been the ultimate act of body hatred, a self-mutilation on par with any other form of pathological self-harm."[2]

I've forced scars upon my body, but my body kept injuries from other things, too, things I never meant to happen. My middle school had these amazing things that my elementary school didn't: tetherballs. If the balls were strung up on the poles at

---

[1] Orchinik, Leah J. Cutting & Self-Injury. (2022). *Psychology (Behavioral Health) at Nemours Children's Health*

[2] Febos, Melissa. The feminist case for breast reduction. (May 11, 2022). *NYTimes*

recess, my couple of friends and I would book it towards them, snagging one before anyone else could. None of us knew the rules of the game; all we knew was that we tried to get the ball wrapped around the rusted pole in its entirety. We'd break into pairs, stand on our respective sides, and slap the ball as hard as we could for the entire half an hour. We tended to play rough, as we were all pretty much tiny tomboys, and one day, a longer nail of mine caught my skin and sliced it open. The cut wasn't very big, maybe a quarter of an inch long, but I watched it. I kept a close eye on it as it healed and then scarred. Back in grade school, it was cool: *I'm so good at tetherball that I got a scar from it!* No, it's sadder: *Wow, my body is scarred after a cut from playing tetherball, of all things.*

A few years later, a scratch from my cat would leave a light scar the length of my entire foot, again, not very gruesome at all. I don't know if it's true or just my mind tricking me, but I swear both of my knees are scarred from falling on them so often in my youth, as many kids do. I have a nearly gone scar on one of my wrists from burning it on a toaster oven when trying to remove my pizza. One of my fingers is permanently broken after I jammed it playing basketball and never got it checked out because it eventually stopped hurting. My right pointer finger is permanently curved because I sucked on it until I was at least ten years old. Some of my toes overlap each other. The sucking-on-my-finger thing also misaligned my jaw, which required braces, a retainer, and then Invisalign to correct.

In her book *Body Geographic*, Barrie Jean Borich writes that "our scars map what's happened between the beginning and the middle, the body flaws we've earned."[3]

---

[3] Barrie Jean Borich. *Body Geographic.* (2013). University of Nebraska Press

The body flaws we've earned—my body is mine because of all it has been through. Sometimes injuries, purposeful or accidental, sometimes a growing body, sometimes a changing body. But there were limits to my efforts. All I could do in sixth grade was rummage for a new bouncy ball every week, test it out, and throw it into the garbage. Once I was out of those little balls, my attempts were out. I felt a war inside me—a part of me said *this isn't harming anyone, it's fine*, but the stronger part of me said *middle school girls don't do this with their bodies.*

I wonder how people become okay or satisfied with their bodies—how much did they have to put their bodies through to get to that point? Will I ever get to that point?

In middle school, I was in both orchestra and chorus. The school was in Maryland, so once a year, our music groups all participated in Music in the Parks—a large music competition in Hershey, Pennsylvania. This all took place in one day, so our itinerary usually went as such:

- Drive the two or so hours to Hershey,

- Perform,

- Change out of performance clothes and into normal clothes on the buses,

- Go to the park for a few hours,

- Attend the ceremony where the results of the competitions were announced, and

- Go home.

After our performances, we'd separate the charter buses between the boys and girls. We'd file onto the buses with our drawstring bags filled with our shorts, tennis shoes, and T-shirts, which were designed by a student every year. Now, buses don't really have private places to change, so everyone just kind of stood within the seats and aisle as they pulled their shirts and pants off. Bag in hand, I would wander to the back of the bus, my grip getting tighter and tighter. We didn't have forever to change, so we all had to be speedy so the boys could get back on and we could get to the park. I'd stand in front of the small bathroom door, waiting for the girl in there at the time to finish. There were bras everywhere, classmates just *so willing* to change in front of other girls, yet I felt confined to this miniature bathroom, with barely enough room to bend down and pull my cargo shorts up. *I can't let them see my body. I'm not like them.* I wasn't as confident as them; my body was odd, something different about it, but I couldn't quite pinpoint what at the time. I know now that it's because I didn't see my body as pretty, my breasts as something to keep—I didn't see myself in this female body.

Even during the regular school day, in gym class, I'd make my way into the shower stalls to change into my clothes while every other just-pubescent girl changed out in the open, again, with bras out in every direction you looked. I wonder what would have happened had I let my classmates see my bra just as I saw theirs. Would I have fit in with them? Would I have been one of them? Would I actually be able to change in the bus with them all as well?

THE IDEA OF SELF-LOVE

One of my childhood best friends didn't shave her legs for the longest time. We met in third grade and kept a solid friendship until eighth grade. We met at an indoor recess period, as she wanted to play *Guess Who?*, and I wanted something to do. We sat across from each other, describing the kooky characters before us how ever our small minds could: *Does your person have hair? No. Does YOUR person have hair? No, too.* Most kids hated indoor recess because there were no slides, basketballs, or mulch to throw at other kids. Inside, we only had board games and dominos. But the two of us spent our time describing bodies, ones with hair, big noses, and green, blue, or brown eyes. The bodies were what one would deem normal, and my friend's legs seemed to stray from that. Her legs were unshaven for the entirety of our friendship. The dark hair coated the feminine legs, something that my own mother, church, and general society had taught me was an abomination, not to be seen. Yet she wore shorter shorts than I did, exposed more skin, and I imagine she did it with confidence. We were too young to probably care too much about our appearances, but my small self could still see the difference; she played at recess, played violin, and visited my house with her unshaven legs out. But unlike what I'd been taught, she didn't care. She became better than me at violin; she found other friends. No one seemed to mind the hair.

The first razor specifically geared towards women was developed and released to consumers in 1915.[1] In her book *A History of Popular Women's Magazines in the United States, 1792-1995*, Mary Ellen Zuckerman writes that in 1904, women's magazines spent over $30 million in advertising. By 1917, after Gillette came into the picture, that number increased to $45 million. This is because money given to magazines and journals for advertising also went to women's magazines. In fact, these magazines "attracted almost a third of the dollars."[2]

The first image advertising Gillette's new ideal showed a small-chested woman at the top of the page; she had a black circle as a backdrop behind her. Her hair was short and curly, and her face pointed towards the reader, her eyes portraying some sense of wanting or lust. Her arms bend at the elbows behind her like she should be using her hands as a pillow to rest. Her pits, arms, and chest are bare, free of hair. Her dress is flowing, but it shows off the skin. It tells women they can be "without embarrassment" if they do the work to have "immaculate underarms." The ad appeals to women's desire to be physically attractive: "sleeveless dresses, the thinnest of silk hose and knee-length skirts make superfluous hair an embarrassment." The ad even came with a coupon for a cream to apply after shaving to keep your skin silky smooth.[3]

A later ad would show a woman in a one-piece suit at the beach, arms again raised and bent behind her head to show off her underarms. The ad asks women, "Are you going to permit unsightly hair on your face, arms, underarms and limbs to spoil the freedom which awaits you at the beach?"[4]

---

[1] Rauner, Samira. How the Beauty Industry Pressured Women Into Shaving. (July 3, 2020). *The Indiependent*

[2] Zuckerman, Mary Ellen. "Marriage of convenience: Advertising and women's magazines." (1998). *A History of Popular Women's Magazines in the United States, 1792-1995*, Greenwood Press, 58-77.

[3] Rauner, Samira. How the Beauty Industry Pressured Women Into Shaving. (July 3, 2020). *The Indiependent*

[4] Ibid

Although I've never read a women's magazine in my life, the effects still linger in television, social media, my surroundings, my parents, and myself.

In high school, girls had to wear long, black dresses for orchestra concerts. As many of us joked, it looked like we were going to a funeral. The day before each concert was maintenance day—I'd shave everything from head to toe to ensure that no body hair was showing. By this point, I'd leaned more towards just wearing longer sleeves so I didn't have to shave under my arms, but for these concerts, the dresses barely had sleeves, so off I went to stand in the shower for over thirty minutes, perfecting a smooth and hair-free body. I had to ensure that I was like all the other girls, no sort of hair showing as I was doused in stage lighting for an hour.

I imagine that the look on my mom's face when I told her that I wanted to start shaving my legs was one of happiness, that her daughter had entered womanhood and was knowledgeable enough to know that women shave their legs. I wonder if she, too, felt a better sense of closeness between the two of us, like I was finally her teenage daughter that she could bond and talk about boys with. I wonder if this bond was severed when I stopped shaving my legs a few years later.

I stopped shaving when I was seventeen because
I am transgender.

HOPE

In late 2014, I sat in the computer room when a video popped up in my recommended list: *Transgender Teens Fall in Love:*

A young couple sits on a raft in the middle of a lake. The young woman wears a white bikini with some blue and purple on it, while the young man wears some colorful swim trunks, exposing his nude chest to the world. The two splash their feet in the water and chit-chat, all while smiling. The two begin to splash about even more—they move the raft slowly. The video cuts to a side-by-side picture of both the girl and the guy when they were younger. They didn't look as comfortable when they were younger. The "before" picture of Katie, the girl, shows a little boy. The boy is smiling, widely, in fact, but it's the wideness of the smile that makes it seem forced like the boy wasn't truly there on the inside. Katie beams now. Her smile is natural, less intense. Yes, she has longer hair and a rounder face, and yes, she's a girl, but it's the smile that shows that she's made her body *hers*.

The video now shows a before and after of Arin, the guy in the trunks. In his before, Arin, too, is smiling, as Katie was. His grin isn't as large and present as hers was. It's more casual. A small smile that he didn't put his whole heart into. His lips are rimmed with a shade of lipstick that any young girl would love, and he has a matching bow slightly hidden in his long, brown hair. Now, his smile, like Katie's, says "home."

Katie now drives by herself. Through the window, the viewer can watch the lush green trees pass by. With a microphone on her shirt, Katie tells us that she is worried for her boyfriend as he underwent major surgery to remove his breast tissue. The green pushes along with the car as she reassures the viewers that Arin is ready for this drastic change. She knows it, and he knows it too. Katie gets out of her car and walks up to the front door of a house. She knocks, and Arin opens with a smile. The couple hugs each other as Katie's excitement escapes from her lips. Once the two release each other, Katie looks eager to feel her boyfriend's designer chest. She does so gently.

The two are in Arin's bedroom now, where, in the safety of his room, he bares his chest with pride. Katie looks on in awe. Arin tells her where he still has some scar tissue, where anesthesia was given, and where the drain holes have now closed up. Arin himself speaks about his chest: *When you're transgender, you learn that your outside doesn't matter; it's what's on the inside. I look in the mirror now, and I just see what I've always seen.*

The couple decides to celebrate Arin's return home with a day out on the lake. Arin drives a white, clean motorboat as Katie sits on the bow in all her glory. Now the couple is kissing—Arin's rainbow-striped shorts match Katie's white Aeropostale bikini. They're back on the raft now, looking into each other's smiling eyes.

I could change. I could be a man. I could be like Arin. Almost instantly, I knew this was my avenue for feeling like me in this body. Being a man will allow me to feel some sort of self-love.

An email I sent to my mom on February 2, 2015:

Dear Mom, I would like to tell you this in person, but it causes me too much stress and anxiety even thinking of it. So I'm just writing you instead. These last few weeks, maybe for a bit over a month even, I have been confused about who I am, as well as questioning some things. This isn't a bad thing, though; everyone has to find who they are in life. But in order to find myself out, I would appreciate it if you would allow me to talk to someone who has no knowledge of me and cannot judge me easily, like a therapist. More specifically, a gender therapist. I feel that talking to someone like this will help me figure a lot out about myself and maybe discover some new aspects as well! I have been wanting to do this since winter break because I believe it will truly help. Parents always want to help their kids however they can, right? It doesn't have to be very expensive and fancy, but just someone well educated and good. I would also like that, for now, if you please do not bring this up in person just yet because, like I said earlier, it gives me a lot of anxiety. I just ask that you would consider and think about this option and not treat me any differently than you already do; I'm still the same! This would all be a great help to me. Thank you.

A response from my mom after I sent that email:

Your dad and I will do whatever we can to help you in any way. It will take a little time to locate someone for you to talk to, but I will let you know when we arrange it. We love you! Mom

But can I live a fulfilling life as a woman?

I tried that, and it didn't work.

I wrote out the monologue from "The Proof of Your Love" and glued it inside my school agenda book:

If I speak with human eloquence and angelic ecstasy but don't love, I'm nothing but the creaking of a rusty gate. If I speak God's word with power, revealing all His mysteries and making everything plain as day, and if I have faith that says to a mountain, "jump," and it jumps, but I don't love, I'm nothing. If I give everything I won to the poor or even go to the stake to be burned as a martyr, but I don't love, I've gotten nowhere. So, no matter what I say, what I believe, what I do, I'm bankrupt without love.

The monologue was an effort in assurance, as other pages of the notebook were filled with lyrics from different songs, ones I cannot listen to even now due to the emotional pain they carry. October 7-11, 2013, reads, *one final fight, for this tonight;* December 2-6, 2013, (my birthday week) reads, *even if I say "it'll be alright," still I hear you say you want to end your life;* May 5-9, 2014, reads, *my heart is starting to accept that I am giving up;* the final week of the school year, June 9-13, 2014, reads, *I don't want to be here anymore.*

But the monologue was ineffective. When I turned to the God I was once so determined to rely on, there was no remorse. If the church had taught me wrong on the subject of women's bodies, was this teaching of reliance wrong too? No amount of God or anything else eased these feelings of worthlessness. But one year after that final week of school, a different discovery would bring me the ease I craved.

HOPE DISINTEGRATED

I sat on the grey couch in our basement that divided the room into two sections: gaming and playing. Smack in the center of that couch, my dinosaur phone beside me, I sweated nervously. My hands gripped the shiny black that controlled the redneck who killed zombies on the TV screen. *PAUSED* emerged in the midst of death as my phone ding-dongs on the storm-cloud couch.

Breathe. My legs stretched naturally as I got up to shut the console off.

The ride to my therapist's office was silent and sweaty. My mom and I entered the waiting room, and my therapist called me in so we could talk before my mom joined us. I sat alone on the leather, staring at the corner of the waiting room, where a table full of children's books sat, yearning to be read—to be heard. I never thought I'd identify with a picture book.

My mom sat across from me, smiling contently. My hands had nothing to sweat on anymore. My heart thrums with each intense beat.

The letter I gave my mom in therapy on July 2, 2015, when I came out to her:

Dear Mom, today I want to tell you something that is very im-portant for you to know. I want to start off by saying that I have found that I am more of a boy than a girl, but I don't want you to think I came up with this overnight. I have been thinking about this for nearly half a year. One event that helped me come to this realization was right around Christmas. I had been very depressed for about a year. Although, I was never fully sure why I was so unhappy. Over winter break, I found out why. I found out that people cannot feel like their sex, and when I did, the depression slowly started to fade. I realized this wasn't weird and that it was how I was feeling. There were many other people who felt how I did, so I decided to embrace who I was. I cut my hair and wore clothes that made me look how I wanted and started to talk with a deeper voice. One way I was able to see if this feeling was true was over the orchestra spring trip. I got to be in Busch Gardens, a place where no one knew how others knew me. During that trip, I was called "he" and "sir" at least three times. Every time this happened, I became so happy, literally smiling. It felt so natural to me. I don't expect you to accept me right away, but I do hope that eventually you will. I just wanted to bring this to your attention so I don't have to hide this part of me. I want to be able to express myself and be comfortable around you.

She looked me in my teary eyes:
We'll never call you that name.

I was at the therapist's office again. My dad and I sat on opposite ends of the couch. The seat in front of him was vacant, and my therapist sat a few feet in front of me, facing us both. We all tried as hard as we could. To me, this was my last chance to be understood—to be loved in my home. My therapist asked him: *If you woke up tomorrow in a woman's body, could you live life that way?*

Of course not, he replied with a scoff.

Words were tossed back and forth. My mom was absent from the meeting. She had refused to attend this session, where we discussed my future surgery. She gave up on trying to understand, and I wasn't going to wait around for her so I could make myself *me*. Her image occupied the empty seat for the whole hour.

Within weeks of injecting testosterone cypionate into my fat, *things* began to grow. Testosterone makes biological males' balls drop, and so when it is given to a female body, the clitoris grows and elongates. Our genitals all start at the same place in the womb; for males, the hole closes, and the balls form, and then the anatomy above the area grows and becomes the penis. For females, the hole stays, and the anatomy remains the same as the clitoris. Since these organs have the same origin, the clit grows, like the penis does in utero, when the body receives testosterone.

It was late at night when I first noticed this bodily change, one I had been anxiously awaiting. I, like most other teenagers, was spending my time browsing porn on any website I could find (fun fact: more testosterone = more of a sex drive). I'd browsed forums online where other female-to-male trans people would exclaim how happy they got when they would see their junk get erect from arousal, and I couldn't wait to see my own do the same—it would be just *that* much closer to being something similar to a penis. Well, this one night, I looked down between my legs and saw it, a tiny head peeking out from the folds of barely darker skin. I took a picture to commemorate the moment. My body was changing again, but in ways I wanted it to now. I had control over my body. But that testosterone alone wasn't enough.

Regardless of this victory, every day for two years, I wore a prosthetic penis to continue to try and fake a sense of bodily autonomy—*Maybe now I'll be even closer to a normal man.* I spent $300+ dollars on the prosthetic itself and a harness to keep it in place, and another $300+ on high-quality underwear to keep it in place all day. The thing was silicone, so when it was hot, it stuck to my skin, rubbing to create friction. It was supposed to give others the illusion of a male bulge, and it was supposed to help *me* pee standing up, like men do. But after wearing it for an hour, I would do anything for a break. It felt like a hot, mildly wet slide rubbing against my downstairs area *all day*. I continued to wear it for two years, insisting it brought me that sweet *comfort* I craved between myself and my body. The injections, wearing that binder for hours on end every day, and wearing that prosthetic helped to an extent, but nowadays, I dread having to force a needle into my skin, and I haven't worn that prosthetic in two years. It still sits at the back of my underwear drawer. Sometimes, I pull the thing out and look at it. I turn it around in my hand, taking note of every crease in the silicon skin. The fake skin tone doesn't even match my own, and as much as this thing *wants* to look like a real penis, it just doesn't. The shaft is too "hard" for a flaccid penis, but it has to be that way so it can be used to pee with. I wonder how many people thought I had an erection when I wore it back in college.

If I couldn't love myself, maybe someone
else's love could satisfy me.

I never let anyone else even *see* my now long-gone breasts, except for two times—the first time was when I dated this guy named Q for maybe two weeks during my first year of college (I use the term "dated" loosely). We met via OkCupid and decided to try going out while I was home for Spring Break. My mom drove me to the Inner Harbor of Baltimore, where we met up. He was a larger guy, Black, with short hair. We were both in college, and he described himself as being open to dating all kinds of people, so I figured it'd work out just fine, given that I was only "socially transitioned" at the time, not having taken any medical steps yet. We wandered around the harbor, ate at a pizza place, and had a fun time, so we scheduled a second date.

Going into this date, our plan was to watch a movie named *Hannibal Rising*, cook some chicken alfredo, and maybe get up to some mild adult fun. Well, what he didn't tell me was that his bedroom was *actually* the living room, so anything we got up to wasn't guaranteed to be behind closed doors. We *did* watch the movie, and afterward, he began to hover his body over mine a bit more, propping himself up with one of his arms. We began to kiss, and it slowly transformed into his tongue slinking its way into my mouth. It felt weird, and I was not a fan. But as we kissed, he slipped his hand under my shirt. Instead of smooth, naked skin, he was met with the mesh texture of my chest binder. Think of it like this: if a sports bra has a bit more compression than a regular bra, then a binder is like a super super *super* sports bra. Those things are so tight and constricting that it's only recommended that people wear them for eight hours maximum, and one even risks broken ribs *every time* you put one on. Q began to rub my chest over my binder and then pulled it up so it bunched up near my collarbone. He slid a hand over my breasts, squeezing gently as his tongue continued to explore. He rubbed and squeezed at them, yet I felt nothing. Maybe *he* enjoyed them, but *I* certainly did not. I felt nothing when he touched them. They didn't feel like something I could take confidence in. They just felt *there*.

How quickly would the little creature be eaten without its transformational skin? What if his body malfunctioned and did not protect him? What if all this, all that I do, does not help me find any self-love? If change is necessary, what do I do when the change is ineffective?

A NECESSARY DESTRUCTION

When I was 22 years old, my mom and I traveled to Washington, D.C., so I could have a surgeon remove my breasts, which I never wanted, as per my medical treatment for gender dysphoria. My mom and I zombied out of the house around 4 a.m., as the surgery was scheduled for 9 a.m., but we had to be at the hospital by 6 a.m. She wasn't happy about my decision, but she agreed to be my transportation to and from. We drove down the two-lane highway that leads right into D.C. She followed me around the hospital as I was ordered to go to the admin desk, then the prep area, just all over that place. I sat in a wheeled hospital bed, separated from all the other patient beds by curtains. A short nurse told me to take my clothes off and hop in, then some other woman came in to do something I don't remember, and then an anesthesiologist came in to explain the process of going under to me as a fourth woman put my IV in. Then, the man himself, Dr. Ramineni, came in to make sure I was all good to go. I laid in that bed for maybe an hour, minimum, before all those people came in, and that *entire* time, my breasts were sweating like it was 90 degrees in that hospital. These were my last moments with them, these mounds I had been taught were things to be accepted, *valued* even, yet also things I had to hide. I no longer wanted them.

Sometimes, I consider what my life would be like now had I kept them. Would I still be wearing my binder every day? Would I have eventually learned to accept my breasts as much as I could? What if more people had touched them? What if

AJ, my now fiancé, had touched them? Would he have liked the soft skin? Would he, too, have played with them under my shirt? What would it feel like to have them flying in every direction as I lay below him while he fucks me roughly? I don't necessarily *miss* those breasts—I just think about them from time to time. For the people with breasts, you know how sometimes you just feel the urge to give them a decent squeeze? I just want to squeeze them again. Maybe it's similar to the single thought people often have before getting a tattoo: *This part of my body will never be naked again.* But instead, my brain is finally comprehending: *I'll really never experience breasts again, in a good or bad way.*

Melissa Febos shared her thoughts before having breast reduction surgery, saying that "it was a bizarre sensation, to look at my breasts for the last time. There would be some of the same tissue, yes, and a new nipple cut from the old one, but the breasts I had spent so many years wishing different, their particular weight, would be gone forever. In the surgical theater, the body is sacred only to its inhabitant. It did sneak up on me, the strange feeling of sacredness, as my surgeon squeezed and measured and scrawled on my breasts with a marker on the morning of my surgery."[1]

Had *my* breasts also been *sacred?*

*What if I had embraced my body like those painted
women in Times Square?*

---

[1] Febos, Melissa. The feminist case for breast reduction. (May 11, 2022). *NYTimes*

I kept pictures of my breasts in my old phone, in the *hidden* folder on Snapchat. They eventually made their way to my old computer when I backed up the phone before getting a new one. Now, those breasts sit in my *photos* on the current phone, unhidden and there for anyone to scroll and see. That same picture is on my surgeon's new website, showing my before-and-after. That day I had them removed, I never thought about ideas of regret or even remembrance. I wanted them gone, and I was happy to do so. But when I look at those pictures, something within me wants to remember what it was like having them. What did it feel like when I rolled over in bed and they would *plop* onto my arm? Could I feel them when I'd bend down to get something off the floor?

Two weeks after my surgery, I had to venture back into D.C. to get my drains and bandages removed. The sterile office air combined with the smell of my body that hadn't taken a proper shower in two weeks. The doctor unclipped the mesh binder, pulled the thick bandages from over my nipples and the longer ones from over my incisions, and pulled the drains out, which felt like fresh, wet spaghetti slapping against my underarm. With everything off, Dr. Ramineni asked, *Would you like to get up and look in the mirror?*

I slid off the chair and shuffled my way over to the mirror, and I was *devastated*. My chest was painted a mix of oranges, yellows, maroons, and purples; one of the incisions was *noticeably* longer than the other, coming to the center of my chest instead of an inch from it; and my nipples, well, they just looked *gross* and as brown as a Hershey's chocolate bar.

I made a BIG mistake, my brain told me.

For the *next* two weeks, I had to dress the nipples to keep them moisturized so they would re-attach themselves, keep bandages over them to protect them as they healed, and apply scar cream to the incisions daily. I also had to keep the compression binder on, so yay for that, I guess. Over those two weeks, the Hershey's brown on my nipples peeled away, exposing the healthy, light pink ones underneath, which had successfully connected back onto the skin (hallelujah!). From there, they began to darken back to their original color.

I watched my body heal itself. *I made it do this*, I thought. *It sure looks horrible, but I also am willing to put my body through anything so I can love it.*

Near the end of my undergraduate run, a friend of mine, Kelsey, stopped shaving her body hair. A self-portrait hung in her dorm room; her portrait self was clad in a fitted burgundy knit tank top that had cream and green stripes across the front. Her body and head tilted to the side a bit, sort of like she was questioning everything you'd say in that room. Her hands were bent above her head, holding a basic, white Polaroid pointed out. With her arms raised, her glorious underarm hair was on full display, complete with hairs sticking out to the side, some curling a tad, and more. But what surprised me was that she looked *gorgeous*.

Walk through a single city in the summertime, or even a college campus, and you'll notice the number of women not caring to shave their body hair. I see a woman with a tank top on walking past the fountain, hair just barely sticking out from under her arms. I see another girl with shorts that end just below the cheeks strutting across the cement path, legs protected by a thin but dark layer of leg hair. The men on campus looked the same: legs, underarms, even facial hair, all out without a care. Everyone looked the same, everyone was equal, and everyone was confident in their selves.

But just one month after my surgery, the day before classes started for the semester, my love for my body backfired. It couldn't handle what I'd put it through. The fluid that would've drained into the, well, *drains*, was now draining into a cavity under my skin. My right side was again a collage of purple and yellow, and this time it had hardened. Knowing my surgeon had been able to drain it before, my two friends, Rose and Kelsey, drove me to the ER to have them do just that. I sat in that bed, my gnarly chest exposed to all three of us, for nearly four hours (and this was before a doctor even came in). The cloth gown became much too warm as my body became more and more anxious. I couldn't stop it. Once someone finally came in, they claimed they couldn't drain it due to legal reasons and *not ruining the surgeon's work*. They called the surgeon, and he said he could see me tomorrow. *I can't get to D.C. by tomorrow; classes start, and it's a four-hour drive minimum.* Instead, all I could do was treat it with a warm compress for a few weeks so that the once-fluid bodily fluid would become fluid again and my body would simply absorb it. I think back to my initial hormone consultation, when the endocrinologist asked me a stream of questions like, *Are you ever wanting to have biological children?* My answer was *no*, but if my answer were to change to *yes*, I'd potentially have to deal with infertility. I knew that when I had my breasts removed, I'd have no way to feed any potential child. *Should I have removed these perfectly healthy body parts?*

I don't know the answer.

I'm sitting at my desk. My back is slouched over slightly because I have horrible posture and don't care enough to correct it. I'm shirtless, fresh out of the gym, my pecs defined seemingly perfectly. I reach a hand somewhere between my back and my side, my *right* side, to be exact. My hand slides forward a bit, towards my astounding pec—but it stops over a bump. You see, breasts don't just sit on the front of your chest; depending on how large they are, some of the fat wraps around sort of under your armpits. When the breasts are removed in a double mastectomy, this includes the fat that wraps around. While this leaves less than 5% of the breast tissue on the chest, sometimes, once everything is stitched back together, the end of the scar that is in that armpit area turns into a teepee or a pyramid; it points to form a "dog ear."

At my three-month check-in with my surgeon, he explained that if I wanted to remove the dog ear within that year, he would do so for free, as I guess it was part of the surgery "package." When he said this, insinuating he wanted some sort of answer or idea from me, I told him, *I have my pecs, and my nipples survived and re-attached to my body with most of their color, so I don't need anything more, and frankly, I'm not up for another medical thing.*

I'm fine without the revision, I told him. And I am, 90% of the time, except when I stand in front of the mirror shirtless after my time at the gym. I flex and, in a way, contort my body in any way that is flattering.

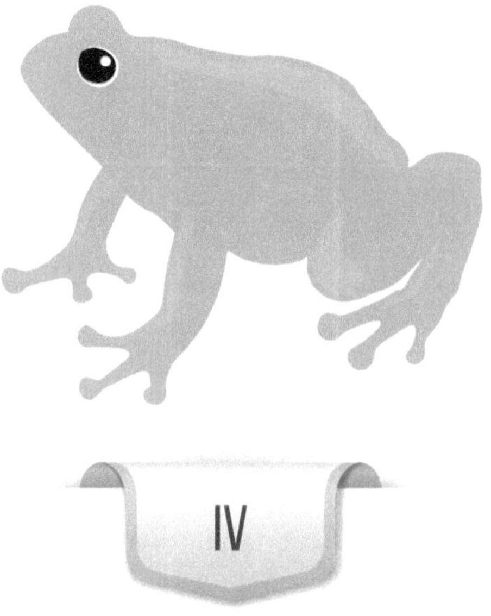

Not all changes are positive—some are both positive and negative. The frog may get slopped into the mouth of a predator at first, but the body spikes tell the predator to drop it, that it's not food. There can be a sense of failure at first, but that's when you try again.

SEX AS BODILY AUTONOMY

In college, I'd approach this taking-back of bodily autonomy through dating. I told myself way back in middle school that I'd let myself date guys when I turned sixteen. Well, I turned sixteen, and there was no line of cute boys dying to date me. So, when I moved three hours east to go to school, I took to all the dating websites I could find. Maybe *sex*, *men*, a *relationship*, was my path to finding this autonomy I longed for.

During that second movie date with Q, the guy I saw during my first college Spring Break, not only did he squeeze at my breasts, but he ventured down under, too.

Nothing goes in, remember? Like I told you.

Oh? Nothing goes in? he repeated as he slid a single finger inside. My body squirmed out of instinct, as it never even had so much as a tampon inside of it. He plunged that finger back and forth, and all I could feel was it rubbing on the rigid walls inside. I wasn't sure what I was *supposed* to be feeling that was so good, but this did *not* feel good. Eventually, he stopped.

Did you finish?

I nodded so I could go home.

I ended it a week later; my first go at sex was *scary*, to say the least—*this is supposed to make people feel good and sexy, but how? It was just uncomfortable, and his dick felt like a wet pickle in my hand. Ew.*

A musing I wrote right after that encounter with Q:

6/11/17

Once the movie was over, I had anticipated the two of use us making some lunch and enjoying it together. That assumption was very far off from what actually happened. Prior to this visit, I had established that I was not comfortable with kissing on the lips or anything entering my body and all beyond that. He had agreed. However, once the movie was over, it began. The man began to kiss at my neck, which I truly didn't mind. As this was going on, his hand slowly made it's its way down my body. He soon made his way into my pants, attempting to slide his fingers inside. I quickly stopped him, telling him that I don't want him to do that to my body.

He looked down at me, his face filled with disappointment and confusion. I told him again to please not try it again, and he expressed to me that he felt let down by my decision. My entire life, I had been taught to please the crowd, which comes with being raised as female. With this mindset, as he later tried once more, I allowed it in a way. I told him to stop it again, but his finger was already inside, so I gave up. I let him take control of me, even though in that moment, my extreme feelings of depression returned. I felt helpless, at the mercy of this man whom I thought I cared for. Once the mindset took control, I had figured I needed to service him. I was the victim, I felt helpless, I wanted to cry. There was no feeling of pleasure, only emotional pain. Once he had relieved himself, I thought it was finally over. However, he started again. I was entered once more, and more trauma made it's its way into my heart. I couldn't do anything to stop it; I had to suffer through the rest of the day.

I lied to him and told him I enjoyed myself when I had done quite the opposite. On my drive home, the dread hot hit me even harder than before. I wanted to break down and cry my life away there in the car, but I had to get myself home. When I got home, a high hit me. My mind tried to repress what I had initially felt. The next day, the dread came back. It was as bad as earlier in my life, so much so that I wanted to hurt myself as I had years before. I was ignored, abused, and raped by this man, and he refused to own up to it.

This guilt and newfound depression would stay with me for life; it would never leave. This trauma would most likely impact my future relationships, and even impact my self-esteem. I would shake whenever he would text me days after, and just thinking about it brought me to tears. My love life is ruined, thanks to one man and one day.

Maybe if I found someone like me, someone else who was trans, I'd find more confidence in my body, and I'd learn to love it. So, a handful of months later, I let Mike, a fellow trans dude, see my breasts. He was the only other person to ever see them. He was large like Q, but he had shoulder-length dreadlocks. We were both in similar spots in our transitions at the time, having been just a handful of months on testosterone, so what could go wrong, right?

Mike and I, both sophomores in college, went to different schools, so he only ever visited me on my campus twice since he had a car and I did not. But he came down for a weekend, and I had a plan—I was going to *seduce* him. That evening he arrived, we promptly made our way to a small hotel on the other side of town. I lived with a roommate in my dorm, so we got a hotel room for *obvious* reasons. We got to the hotel room, changed into our PJs, and spread out on the bed. He laid longways in front of the pillows, and I laid the same in front of him. We opened up my laptop, browsing our options on Netflix. We decided on *Cat Woman* for the night. At this point, I was in my underwear and a long-sleeved button-up. When Mike had wandered to the bathroom to get changed, I'd unbuttoned my shirt a bit, enough that my breasts were *just barely* visible to him. As we lay there, he put an arm around me, keeping me close against his body. I imagined him slipping a hand into my unbuttoned shirt, leaning forward to kiss the back of my neck. Instead, he fell asleep halfway through the movie. I closed the laptop and fell asleep, too.

The next night, my dorm mate was gone, so Mike stayed the night with me in my tiny twin bed. Tonight, we watched another movie, *V for Vendetta*. The movie is looooong, so by the time it finished, it was maybe 2 a.m. It was then that Mike began to kiss me, then make out with me, like Q had months before. He slipped his hand under my shirt, but there was no binder in the way. He pulled my shirt up, and I watched him set a hand on my left breast, squeezing it gently. The skin and fat slid around in his hand before the nipple poked through, then the areola. He brought his lips close and encased them around the pink skin. I was silent, unfeeling. He continued to the other side. I could have sworn that after his mouth played with them, these small bumps, almost pimple-like, appeared around my nipple, covering the areola. I'd look at them in the mirror, hold them. Something was different—I couldn't get that feeling of his mouth out of my head, and not in a good way. I hated that he liked them. I hated *them*. That's when I decided I 101% wanted them gone and that maybe sex *wasn't* the best way to get back my control.

The Washington Post reported that "from 1901-1924, adults ... averaged three partners" throughout their *entire* adulthood; Baby Boomers averaged 11 partners; Generation X averaged 10; Millennials are expected to average about eight. Additionally, "between 2006 and 2008, 11 percent of teenage girls and 14 percent of teenage boys reported having sex before age 15— compared to 19 percent and 21 percent in 1995."[1] Young people now tend to have sex at older ages and fewer partners within

---

[1] Paquette, Danielle. Why Millennials have sex with fewer partners than their parents did. (May 6, 2015). *The Washington Post*

a lifetime. I was worried. Worried I wouldn't ever find a real boyfriend. I was already two deep, and neither of them lasted. I decided then that maybe my mind was right; maybe I wasn't cut out for this dating thing. It felt like these men didn't want me romantically, instead only sexually. It was a priority for everyone but me.

When I was having sex with these men, I was giving my body up to them. If growing up with sex education through my church had taught me one positive thing, it's that sex is valuable. Ever since I was young, I have told myself that anyone I have sex with will be meaningful. If I'm giving these men nearly free roam of my body, inside and out, it should be meaningful, right? I always wanted any moment a man uses my body to be meaningful, special, like a fairy tale.

But this sex had not been what I had imagined. There had been no pleasure like the scenes in movies, no romantic soundtrack, either. I felt like I was a body, not a person.

I tried another approach.

There was one time in my undergrad when I thought that maybe I'd feel more manly by pegging a guy. I'm a smaller guy, only 5'3 and around 150 pounds, so picturing this in my own head now makes me chuckle. There is *no* way I can see myself topping a regular guy. But a few years ago, I could. *Real men are tops*, I told myself. *They're controlling, in charge, all that dominant stuff.* I hit up some random guy up on Grindr, told him about my wishes, and he agreed to volunteer. We made plans for him to come to my dorm around 10 p.m., and all day, my heart was racing. Part of me wanted this guy to come over so I could try this experience, but a louder part of me said that this would throw me into emotional distress for days or even *weeks*. All my previous tries at sex, with Q and Mike, were failures. But maybe this was it. Maybe this was my fix.

I waited in my room, unable to do any homework in the meantime. I sat on the bed, trying to picture myself behind a man larger than me in every way, plunging a fake dick in and out of his ass. 10 p.m. came and went, and I continued to wait. By 11 p.m., I figured he wasn't coming, so I stripped my body of any clothes and crawled into bed. The fake dick still sat on my desk.

The next morning, I got a message from the guy: *Sorry about last night, fell asleep.* I wanted to tell him that it was okay, that we could arrange for another day and time, but I didn't respond, and I deleted the account not a minute after getting that message.

The Daily Universe writes that "these types of interactions [hookups] have been on the rise since the 1920s with the invention of cars and movie theaters ... There was a spike in the 1960s due to the widespread availability of birth control and gender-integrated parties and events."[2]

However, "of 1,468 undergraduate students who reported a variety of negative consequences of hookups: 27.1 percent felt embarrassed, 24.7 percent reported emotional difficulties,

---

[2] Barratt, Jenna. Studies show negative effects of hookups. (February 10, 2016). *The Daily Universe*

20.8 percent experienced loss of self-respect and 10 percent reported difficulties with a steady partner."[3]

"BYU commitment therapist Ben Salazar said it is impossible for hookups to maintain a sense of casualty. 'There is no such thing as casual when it comes to a makeout,' Salazar said. 'Kissing involves so much more than two people locking lips.' He said kissing triggers all types of physical responses. According to *Women's Health* magazine, salivary glands start producing more spit, blood flow increases to certain areas in the body and the brain releases more oxytocin. Oxytocin shapes the neural circuitry of trust and trust adaptation in humans. Oxytocin is released into the body during intimacy and touching according to *Oxytocin Central*. The hormone increases feelings of trust and attachment between individuals."[4]

It was my first semester after starting grad school in the fall of 2020. I had lost my virginity to a man who, it turns out, didn't even like me in the same way I liked him, in *that* way, and as someone who once thought that sex maybe just wasn't for me, after that night, I learned that sex is *very* much for me.

I met Cody on Grindr; he was a hint taller than me, lean, and had a sort of early Justin Bieber-esque haircut. He invited me to his apartment one night. I sat on the couch beside him, eventually leaning my head on his shoulder as we watched *Hereditary*. The movie is a long one, so it must've been close

---

[3] Ibid

[4] Ibid

to midnight by the time it ended. The last hour or so of the movie, he stopped responding to my little talkings. He seemed to scowl towards the TV a little, annoyed that it wasn't over. I asked him how it was after it ended, and he just responded with, *Okay*. The next day, he apologized for his behavior at the end of the night, that it just happens when he's tired. I forgave him. At least once a week, I spent a night at his apartment. We made dinner together, went shopping together, and watched *Grey's Anatomy* together. I liked this guy more than the other guys I'd been involved with. He was kind, cute, funny. One day, he told me we could have sex that night—

The movie ended. The two of us got up from his couch, me untangling myself from him. It was late at night. We wandered into his bedroom. He put another movie on, to my confusion: *Wait, so are we not doing, ya know, that?* I thought to myself. I gave him a firm kiss on the lips once we'd gotten into bed, my body and mind gearing up for what was to happen after. He lay there, watching the movie for maybe half an hour before he reciprocated.

I'd lay in his bed beside him, smiling over at him, worming closer. It was like trying to be affectionate to a gingerbread man. I'd come over; we'd watch tv, never cuddling all the while; eat dinner; and go to bed. If I hinted at wanting sex, he'd simply say, *I'm not that into sex*. Sometimes, he had me drive him to do errands. I gave him rides to work in the Minnesota winter, when there was more snow than road, and he'd kiss me goodbye as he left my car. I asked him again when we would officially be dating; I got the same answer every time—*I don't know*. I'd find out months later that instead of being intimate with me, he opted for random Grindr guys, all while still giving me kisses every time I dropped him off at work.

No matter how much I told him that I wanted to have sex with him again, that I *loved* him, he wanted to remain friends—

with benefits? He'd still kiss me and make sexual jokes, but no, we were *just friends*. I held onto the hope of a relationship with him for so long, until December of that same year.

Sex was a means of finding a source of *pride* for my body after my breasts had been tainted by mouths and hands and after my breasts had been removed and my chest was left with prominent scars.

I offer my bodily autonomy; I receive a sense of value.

I was back in Maryland, visiting my family for the first winter break of my grad school program, when a guy, Stephen, hit me up on Grindr. *Trans men are SO hot,* he told me. We arranged for him to pick me up from my parents' house, as I did not have my own vehicle while I was visiting, and I'd spend the night at his place. Come a few hours later, he picked me up, and we made our way toward Fort Meade. We pulled off the highway, booked it across when traffic wasn't coming, ventured through some woods, and down a now unused street to an abandoned asylum. He'd explored this place before, and at this point, I was up to doing anything to get some dick, so I agreed. We wandered around the property, admiring the graffiti of knock-off Disney characters on the walls and jumping over puddles of water, all while trying to avoid security. There wasn't security actually on the property, but one guy with a van sat at an entrance/exit at the perimeter. We soon stumbled across the van, so we wandered back towards the center of the area to lay low for a bit. He'd brought a backpack with him, and it held a soft blanket. He laid it down on a concrete slab just on the other side of a blown-out wall with crumbled brick and shattered glass at the base. He sat down, legs open just enough for me to fit. I sat down in his lap, and his lips began to kiss at my neck, and his hand started to wander my body. Although it was the middle of winter, probably around 40 degrees, he eventually slid my pants to my ankles. I can't recall exactly what he said or any wording he used, but something clicked in my head when he told me that he thought I was attractive, and then even more so when he complimented certain parts of me.

If *he* liked my body how it was,
maybe *I* could like it how it was, too.

Maybe I could be more than just a body.

When are we just a body?

1. After any type of disaster, *crews are still searching for bodies.* They're not searching for *people*; they're looking for *bodies.*

2. After someone has died of natural causes. At my call-center-for-funeral-homes job, nurses would tell me, *I have a body ready for pickup,* for eight hours straight. There's no more person in the body; it's just bone, organs, muscles, skin—

3. When I hooked up with a guy whose name I didn't even know because I was lonely and freshly "de-flowered" and wanted to experience more of the sexual world. He was just a body to satisfy a need.

Like I said, I don't even remember his name. I think it started with a "G." Gavin? Greg? Gordon? Doesn't matter. It was my first year in grad school, my first year living states away from my parents—I had a chance to explore my desires, my sexuality, and this body I had avoided for most of my life so far. I drove home that night—it was only five-something in the evening, but the sun was steadily descending. Maybe halfway through the two-hour drive, I called my friend Sam:

I feel weird.

Weird how? Did something happen?

Well, after the sex, he asked me to be his boyfriend. I didn't think he was cute at all, so of course, I said no. But doing a random hookup ... it felt weird.

Well, maybe it's just not for you?

Maybe ...

The guy whose name started with a "G" messaged me just one day prior to the hookup. Some people are convinced that either no one wants to sleep with transgender people or the people who do fetishize them. That's BS. I've never had a problem finding someone who's interested in me, and so what if they're into trans people specifically? Everyone's got preferences and different types. But the premise of this hookup was simple: I wanted what he had, and he wanted what I had.

In hookup culture, we're bodies. We bodies have needs, needs that other bodies are to fulfill. The American Psychological Association reports that the effect is like a treatment for loneliness: "those with more depressive symptoms and greater feelings of loneliness who engaged in penetrative sex hookups subsequently reported a reduction in both depressive symptoms."[5] But this works in opposite ways, too: "participants who reported fewer depressive symptoms and fewer feelings of loneliness who engaged in penetrative sex hookups subsequently reported an increase in both depressive symptoms and feelings of loneliness."[6] But what if you don't fall into either of these categories? My hookup brought about neither happiness nor loneliness—just emptiness. I didn't like being just a body.

The hookup day went like this: I woke up, went to the gym, ate a small lunch, drove two hours to some town I didn't know the name of in northern Minnesota, sucked off some guy whose name I didn't know, got my insides rearranged, and drove the two hours home. We were just two bodies, satisfying each other. The creaking of his bed was endless, and his bedroom was too warm—do people really do this nearly every day? Did *I* want to resort to these sorts of relations with mildly attractive guys?

Can I find a real relationship? One built on more than just sex? One where I am more than a body for someone to use?

I stared out the window at the town below as the man whose name I did not know thrust into me. There were people at the gas station, cars pulling into pumps and back out onto the main road. They're not bodies out there. Those are people filling up their cars with gas, going home to families after work.

---

5. Garcia, J. R., Reiber, C., Massey, S. G., & Merriwether, A. M. (2013, February 1). Sexual hook-up culture. Monitor on Psychology, 44(2). https://www.apa.org/monitor/2013/02/ce-corner

6. Ibid

I wanted that; I wanted to have sex, romance, a partner.

I met AJ at a grocery store job I had, but *also* on Grindr. First, I met him at work—

I was at my job, working in the online orders department. It was about 9 p.m., so I was just finishing up the last few orders of the night and getting things ready for the team in the morning. As I examined all our varieties of orange juice, I noticed one of the service managers making his way over to me. He stopped and smiled at me when, out of nowhere, he asked me, *Hey, Aarron, wanna see my Nips?* I paused, confused. He pulled out two small caramel candies labeled *Nips* and set them in my hand. *Now go show someone YOUR Nips,* he followed up with before wandering off.

On Grindr—

I was at work. It was 10 a.m. on January 9, 2021. My phone *pinged* the Grindr tone in my pocket. I reached in and pulled it out, just to check if it was the same forty-year-old man who messaged me every week (and every week his message got ignored). There was no name on the profile, but it read, *Keep it classy,* instead. I'm *horrible* with remembering faces, so when AJ's pictures showed up in my inbox, I ignored it; *I'll get to this when I'm home.*

Well, I got home and immediately pulled my phone back out. I read the message this time, my heart honestly stopping when I read, *Hey, Aarron, I didn't expect to see you on here.* Okay, who is this guy, and how does he know my name? Do I know him from somewhere? I waited to respond, and I tried to run through my list of faces in my mind. I couldn't find him.

Who is this? Do I know you?

It's AJ from work.

There went my heart again: *This is bad—Is this against the rules—Wait, he's one of my managers—This is not good; this is a bad idea—I CANNOT fuck my manager—*

But we talked about work, life, small-talk things. We talked about the new trolley carts we just got for the online orders, behemoths that were too big and difficult to maneuver. We'd wean ourselves out of work talk, and he'd type, *So, enough about work,* but we'd just get right back to talking about work. Within a few hours, the conversation got more *spicy.* By the end of the day, AJ asked me, *Oh, so you don't want me to pin you onto my bed and fuck you?* in his sassy tone I'd come to love.

I posted, *Is it a good idea to date my work manager?*
on Snapchat.

Someone responded with,
Do NOT fuck your manager, never turns out well.

I fucked my manager.

We sexualize some bodies but glance over others. Types. My type fell into two categories: 1) the types of guys I wanted as a boyfriend and 2) the types of guys I wanted to be. If you asked my college friends what my type is, heck, if you asked my *own* fiancé, he could all tell you that my taste in men is *basic twinky white boys.* And that goes for both types. Ironically, my fiancé is very much *not* a basic twinky white boy.

Katherine Wu of Harvard University explains that attraction, lust, and attachment, these three aspects, come together to form feelings behind *love* and behind the types of people we are into. Lust is obviously tied to sexual gratification and humans' instincts to reproduce. The hypothalamus is the part of the brain that stimulates the production of sex hormones, both testosterone and estrogen; when we look at someone attractive, our brain is stimulated, and we feel *lust*. Attraction relates more to the reward aspects of our brain; dopamine, a chemical produced by the hypothalamus, is what controls when we feel good. When we spend time or have sex with someone we find attractive through *lust*, we release this dopamine (as well as norepinephrine) and feel *attracted* to them. Being attached to someone is the basis of any relationship. The hypothalamus produces both oxytocin and vasopressin, both "precursors to bonding." So, we feel this "bonding" when we are *attached* to someone.[7]

---

[7] Wu, Katherine. Love, Actually: The science behind lust, attraction, and companionship. (2017). *Harvard University Graduate School of Arts and Sciences*

SEX AND LOVE AS BODILY AUTONOMY

AJ lay across his couch, his head resting on an armrest. I laid my own head down on his chest—I fit perfectly. Our heads were turned towards the TV, an old-school anime playing. AJ is a naturally warm guy, so after a bit, I decided to pull my shirt off. His hands rested above my three-year-old nipples, ones that *didn't* come with weird pimple-bumps from that night, slowly sliding back and forth.

I couldn't really feel much. After I had my double mastectomy in 2019, I lost most of the feeling in my chest. When the surgeon cuts your chest open to pull out all the fat and mammary glands, he has to sever nerves that are hidden within all that. My surgeon also sized down my nipples to that of an average male and a size that would be more proportionate to my future pec muscles—they went from a little larger than a quarter to about the size of a dime-ish. That removal and re-connection also came with more severed nerves. Some nerves *will* reconnect, but some won't. Some reconnect a little awkwardly—I'll touch above my nipple and feel it in some other area of my chest, even on the other muscle.

But where AJ touched, I couldn't really feel it. He moved his hands lower, onto my nipples, and again, nothing. He ran his fingers over the bumpy, curved scars that followed the bottom of my pecs, where the scars could hide with ease. He slid and rubbed them with his soft, gentle touch.

And I could feel all of it. It felt good, relaxing. For the first time in my life, I wanted a partner to touch my chest more.

A text I sent to AJ one day:

This is gonna sound weird, or at least, it does in my head

But I like the feeling of your hands when they be touching like pretty much where my scars are

I understand

You do?

Yes

I wanted him to touch those scars again, to slide a hand under my shirt one day as he kissed me. Maybe he'd grab the back of my head or hold the side of my face, too. I was free of that 3 a.m. night with Mike, free of those perceived blemishes on my original areolas and the thoughts they had left behind. I had new blemishes, *scars*, that *I* liked more than those bumps, and better yet, both me *and* AJ liked those scars.

Another scar, my adoption, was never kept a secret from me. When I came home from elementary school upset that kids were making fun of me, my parents chuckled and said that I should just tell them that at least my parents *chose* me. Even touchy details of my adoption were told to me, like how my birth mother had a number of abortions before I was born; like how I was born two months early, in December of 1997 rather than February of 1998, and when my parents requested a little girl born specifically in 1997, there I was as an option; like how my birth records list a number of *conditions* I had at birth—*Don't worry,* my mom assured me, *they stretched the truth a little to diagnose you with these things so you could get a spot in the orphanage. Kids had to have these things to go there*—like how it was noted that I had mild *speech dysfunction* at birth. When my dad tells me, *You sure are lucky to live in America; I can't imagine you could do this* [transition] *in Russia,* I realize that maybe there is some being or force out there that put me in my birth mother and set everything in motion. Maybe I had to acquire these scars— maybe I had to hate my body—before I could learn to appreciate it.

A list of things I see wrong with my body:

My thinning hair,

My facial hair that grows in all patchy,

My shoulders that never seem broad enough,

My stomach that is too fat,

My hands that cannot even hold a full-sized burrito,

My hips that curl inwards,

My pelvis that holds all the fat and is much too wide,

My ass that works great for sitting but is again too big, and

My feet that cannot fit in normal men's sizes (men's size 6—not many men's shoes come in a size 6).

Dislike of our young bodies follows us into adulthood.

We lay in bed in our hotel room as we were visiting my family in Maryland for Christmas. I rolled on top of AJ and began to kiss his lips. I held his cheek, staring into his eyes with a smile. We'd spent all day at my parents' house with them, my older brother, younger sister, and my uncle and aunt. *I* was glad to have some alone time with him, but I hadn't thought of the idea that maybe *he* was tired and wanted to rest and play some video games. My mind told me this: *It's Christmas, an important day, so to celebrate, you NEED to have sex with him.* I'd convinced myself of this outcome, and so when he simply said he wanted to relax to recharge his battery, my brain and my body broke down.

I went still, couldn't move. I could only cry as my brain immediately began to tell me that AJ wasn't attracted to me or that he didn't love me anymore. I couldn't speak, couldn't force the words out that I wanted to tell him. *He doesn't want you—he doesn't even want your body. You harmed your own body, and for what? You still can feel half of your chest. What's the good in this mutilation if your body can't even function normally?*

ON THE MEDICALIZATION OF A BODY

Functioning normally—once upon a time, I would have preferred the opposite, a cylinder of skin that is supposed to resemble a biological penis but has no feel or proper function.

For a long time, I thought I needed more surgeries. I'd had my double mastectomy (male-ifying my chest), and so I felt the need to get genital surgery (to male-ify my genitals). My mind was at war—if you're a transgender *man*, then you should want to be as close to *man* as possible, even if it meant destroying my fully-functioning genitalia that I was on the fence about. While I was contemplating this more intense course of action, complete with getting quotes from the Johns Hopkins website, I started to consider altering the look of my genitalia in more minimal ways.

How can I become confident in these parts
that I like but don't LOVE?

"Bottom surgery," the slang name for phalloplasty, is when the vagina is sealed up and is replaced by a man-made "penis." Unlike with a double mastectomy, this surgery is often three surgeries minimum, depending on what all is being done. You can have testicular implants or opt out of them; you can have a head constructed or opt out again; you can lengthen your urethra or opt out. To get as close to a real penis as possible, the following is done[1]:

- Creating the penis;

- Lengthening the urethra so you are able to stand to urinate;

- Creating the tip (glans) of the penis;

- Creating the scrotum;

- Removing the vagina, uterus, and ovaries;

- Placing erectile and testicular implants; and

- Skin grafting from the donor tissue site.

Johns Hopkins describes this general procedure as "customizable," like it's getting a new nose. They make this intense, not medically advanced procedure sound just *lovely*.[2]

There are also multiple ways to get a skin graft, which also affects the look of the "penis"[3]:

1. Radial Forearm Free Flap (RFF), where the skin, fat, nerves, arteries, and veins are taken from your forearm and used to construct the "penis;"

2. Anterolateral Thigh Flap (ALT), where the skin, fat, nerves, arteries, and veins are taken from the leg; and

---

[1] Liang, Fan M.D. Phalloplasty for Gender Affirmation. *Johns Hopkins Medicine*

[2] Ibid

[3] Ibid

3. Musculocutaneous Latissimus Dorsi Skin Flap (MLD), where the skin, fat, nerves, arteries, and veins are taken from the side of your back.

All of these procedures leave behind scars much nastier than any I would ever even *purposefully* give myself. The scars look like those of severe burn victims, the skin ending up red and bubbly.

The outcome? A tube of skin that cannot get hard on its own, like a real penis can, cannot ejaculate like a real penis, and has minimal sensation, *unlike* a real penis.

Ryan James, a now-27-year-old FtM started taking hormones at 17, had his breasts removed at 19, had a hysterectomy at age 20, and finally had phalloplasty in 2020 at age 25. In a TikTok video, he tells younger trans men that if they feel that their bottom dysphoria is so negative that they would rather off themselves, to "please, please, please consider other options" first. He tells viewers that this procedure, or the multiple surgeries involved with the process, are not medically advanced enough, that "it isn't suitable for anyone." He describes his initial consult as *off*—when he asked the surgeon to show him before and after pictures, the doctor was hesitant to do so. To clarify, he *is* glad he transitioned, and he's glad to be *him*, but he would rather have not done this to his genitals. Ryan also claims his sexual partner count has gone down since this surgery, too, because he doesn't have much feeling down there anyway. He says that he was *promised* to have full sensation, but unsurprisingly, he does not. He is also amazed/annoyed that he *still* is not done with constructing the phallus in its entirety (he can't even pee out from the tip). He was promised this perfect life, and he received the opposite.[4]

According to a 2021 study done by the Society for Evidence-Based Gender Medicine, out of the 237 total participants (92% of them were assigned female at birth), two-thirds of those assigned female at birth transitioned socially and one-third transitioned socially and medically. Among the one-third who medically transitioned, 46% received gender-affirming surgeries. The average age of transition was 18, but some participants did so *before* turning 18. "On average, detransition occurred roughly 5 years after transition was initiated," and "the participants' decision to detransition was most often tied to the realization that their gender dysphoria was related to other issues (70%), health concerns (62%), and the fact that transition did not alleviate their dysphoria (50%)."[5]

When I went to the surgeon's office for my initial mastectomy consultation, a nurse with a clipboard and pen in hand sat on a stool in front of my armchair, her legs crossed in a very stereotypical "business boss lady" sort of way.

Why do you want to get this surgery?

Wearing a binder is painful every day, and I want society around me to not even question if I'm a guy when looking at me.

What do YOU want to see when looking at yourself?

My last thought before going under?

---

4. Scarcella, Arielle. "Bottom (PENIS) Surgery Ruined My Life": Trans Man Tells All. (2022). *YouTube*

5. Detransition: A Real and Growing Phenomenon. (2021). *Society for Evidence Based Gender Medicine*

*I hope this is **really** the right decision.*

But that was a small thought then. It was passing. After two or three weeks, the thought was long gone. The first time that thought came back, I was scared. I'd removed my breasts, my parents had finally come around, I found the man I wanted to be with forever, and then all of a sudden, I questioned the last six years of my life. I wondered where I'd be if I had stayed in a woman's body, if I had learned to love my breasts.

The Women's Forum of Australia considers that "their [the detransitioned women's] transition stories are variations on a strikingly repetitive theme: undiagnosed mental issues, trauma, peer group 'encouragement' to transition, with no questions asked by the therapists who prescribed medication. Their detransition stories are also similar: unresolved ongoing mental issues now compounded by medical and surgical damage to their bodies, feelings of bitterness towards the therapists who failed to safeguard their welfare and experiences of rejection from the 'trans community' they formerly called home."[6]

One woman who detransitioned describes
her transition process as a *cult*.[7]

For a split second, as I consider *what if I had stayed a woman and learned to love that womanly body,* I also consider the idea of

---

[6] INCREASING NUMBERS OF DETRANSITIONERS CALL INTO QUESTION THE "AFFIRMATION ONLY" APPROACH. (2022). *Women's Forum Australia*

[7] Ibid

detransitioning. I feel that I should've just learned to love my body and avoid all the physical and emotional strain I went through. But I know I couldn't have. Gender dysphoria caused me to hate my female body, to hate what I was born with. A couple years of anguish is better than a whole life of it.

The Women's Forum Australia continues: "Even if medical transition works out well for some, when no care is taken with individual diagnosis, when patients are rushed onto hormones and surgery without any investigation of the aetiology [cause] of their distress, the risk of prescribing medical solutions for non-medical problems increases."[8]

*Could I have lived a fulfilling, stable, and
healthy life as a woman?*

Talk therapy is reported to have a "track record of reorienting 80–95% of dysphoric children to their biological sex."[9]

Could I have found an easier solution to my hatred of my body?

In 2015, I was willing to do *anything* to be as close to a biological man as I could. I was prepared to change my body in ways that I couldn't go back on, through hormones and chest surgery, all at the not-actually-very-adult ages of 19 and 21. I bet in 2015, I would have been ready to mangle my genitals. Had

---

[8.] Ibid

[9.] Ibid

I gone through with my research on those surgeries, I would have *never* been able to one day love my body.

Taz Connell, a tattoo artist, was sexually abused by the owner of a restaurant he worked at. He started to drink regularly and was in and out of hospitals due to self-harm and suicide attempts. But when Connell began to cover his body in tattoos, his life began to change. He explains that "that feeling that I got from getting tattooed kind of soothed the inner demons, if you will, of wanting to self-harm" and that "I now use that as a tool when I start to feel myself slipping back into old habits." The body modifications gave him something to focus on during the healing process, and they're something he *definitely* wouldn't want to ruin in the end; they're *art*. Renee Hudson, the shop owner of Picton Tattoo, explains, "I do find that it's something that people turn to, that they may not have turned to in the past … and if they didn't have this form of expression, they may have gone down the path of doing more unhelpful things like self-harming and not dealing with things in a constructive way."[10]

I considered other options—what simpler action
could I take to help myself love my body?

Instead of destroying my genitals, I paid a kind man to shove a needle through them. I was sitting on a leather-y bed/table in a tattoo-and-piercing shop. A man with shoulder-length dark hair sat in front of the bed and between my legs, which were garmentless and spread open for him to take in. He showed

---

[10.] McLennan, April. Taz's tattoos are a creative 'coping mechanism'—and may have saved his life. (August 3, 2022). *ABC Australia*

me his hands before explaining that he'd slide them down to my crotch. His gloved fingers poked around a bit before he used a purple Sharpie to place a single dot. He reached to his left and rolled a tray over that was holding all types of mad-scientist-looking instruments. He stood back up so I could see his hands, and he showed me the thin needle and the metal tube he'd be using. He explained: *I'm going to lift the skin up slightly so I can slide this tube underneath it. Then I'll put the needle through the skin and into this tube so I don't nick anything important;* he said this with a smile and a chuckle. This metal tube hurt more than the actual needle going through my skin; he had to keep the skin tight so he could push the needle through, but the tube was thick, and forcing thick, cold metal into a small space while increasing the tension in the skin was unpleasant. He moved his hands again with another announcement, gently placing the needle on the soft skin. He pushed with force, but it was gentle at the same time. He ran the needle through the tube and put the bar in the fresh hole, screwed the ball onto the top, and then pulled the bar up slightly to screw on the second ball.

I sat up to take a look as the piercer explained the aftercare to me. We began to talk about the stigma behind genital piercings:

It's crazy that piercings, especially genital ones, are sooooo taboo, like why? It's like pierce your ears, that's fine, but anything that's normally hidden is off limits? Like we gotta do what makes us happy, ya know? The societal stigma is just unreal! The piercer told me.

AJ held me close to him, one hand resting on my waist as we lay in his bed. He started to kiss just behind my ear, just barely breathing against it, too. He moved his body closer to mine; I could feel him against the entire backside of my being. He began to list off parts of my body that he loved: *your cute little lips—your curvy hips—your tummy—your adorable little piercing.* He was attracted to me, to my body, even the modified parts, so I felt confident in myself, too. I just needed someone to show me I could be loved.

FINDING COMFORT IN A BODY

When I allow AJ some of my autonomy, *my self*, I wonder how much of it he takes. Does he only take the parts he likes? The parts that are positive? The parts that are normal?

It was the night before his brother's wedding. We needed the sleep that night, as we were both going to be a pair of wedding lackeys the next day. We lay in bed, and I'd fallen asleep on his chest and into some sort of nightmare. He tells me that when this happens, my body twitches just slightly and I might make some whimpery noises. In my sleep, I felt a gentle hand on my cheek, then heard a whisper: *Aarron, wake up. Aarron. It's okay, wake up.* My eyes opened. AJ's eyes seemed to glow towards me, even if the lights were off and the blinds shut. We looked at each other for a moment.

What's up? My eyes began to water—not out of sadness, but out of *memory*.

I had a dream that hadn't shown up for years; I'm not even sure why now. But I was pulled over on the side of the highway, on that bridge we passed going towards my parents' church when we visited Maryland. I was standing on the edge of it.

Pause.

That was my plan back in high school, when—

He slung his arms around me and pulled me as physically close to him as possible (I was nearly swallowing his chest hair). I listened to his heartbeat inside of him. He took one of my arms, brought my wrist to his lips, and gave it a kiss. He didn't say a word. He took my other arm and kissed it as well. He gave me a good squeeze close to his chest for good measure.

His body is comforting. It's easier to love *his* body than to love my own. I see all the flaws all over myself, but *him, AJ?* I tell him that his body is great, just the way it is. But why will I not believe him when he tells me the same?

Because we all know what our own bodies have been through. We've seen all the little scrapes we got on our knees from traumatic injuries (purposeful or not) when we were little. I had to watch my own hand rip apart the scab that was forming over an old self-inflicted cut with a new toothpick. I had to see what my chest looked like freshly out of a major surgery. When AJ looks at me, he doesn't see *any* of that in his head.

He just sees *me.*

But he does see that dog ear. Heck, he wasn't even fazed when he slid his fingers inside of me and they came out *caked* in blood because of my IUD. He got up, rinsed his hands off, brought me a small towel so as to not get blood on the bed, and gave me a squeeze. He sees all this and yet *still* takes my offering of my autonomy.

I give him my bodily autonomy, and I get a loving fiancé, but what else? Sometimes, I give him myself in the form of a long hug after his workday, and he grips my torso and lifts me into the air, not letting me down until he gets a kiss. Other times, he grabs the Velcro cuffs from his drawer and uses my body how he pleases. He does all this, yet I still think about the words of my past, of the white scars across both of my wrists and thighs, of the body I disdain. But when he takes some of that body for himself, he gives it the love it deserves, the love I cannot give it.

A blogger suggests that "when the love we have obtained doesn't distract us from ourselves enough, we jump ship. We break up. We divorce. We try to find someone new who will fill that hole inside of us. We get bored or scared. We leave. Then the cycle starts again."[1]

Maybe this is what AJ does for me—distracts me
from those parts of me I strive to hide and forget about.
He loves me, *including* those parts.

The blogger goes on to suggest that the reason we use love to "escape ourselves" is because "growing up, we were conditioned to believe that romantic love was the greatest pursuit of life. From the tender age of two or three, we were read fairy tales that depicted princes and princesses falling in love and eventually getting married." This reinforcement of love as the ultimate goal continues as adults through books, movies, television, etc. Love is also a *magical* feeling: "Life suddenly feels magical and awe-inspiring again. Anything feels possible. Tidal waves of joy wash over you. You feel warm, tingly, elevated, and drunk all at once. Optimism replaces your negative outlook on life—you feel like a new person!" When the love we find does not help us escape, we look elsewhere.[2]

---

[1] Why We Use the Search For Love to Escape Ourselves. (2021). *lonerwolf.com*

[2] Ibid

But what about love as *a relief?*

A relief from self-hate, from thinking you're unattractive from thinking no one could ever love you and what your body has become.

Not only does AJ embrace my body in as many ways as he wants, but I also decided after a few months of our relationship that I should, too. The starting point was to make sure I kept it safe and baby-free.

CHOSEN PAIN AS SELF-LOVE

Being pregnant was never something I'd been fond of, even when I *was* living as a woman. So, what did I do when I wanted to be freely intimate with my boyfriend but not risk housing a fetus? I arranged to have my everything (PCP, OBGYN, Endocrinologist, and more) doctor force a "T" piece of plastic into my cervix to smack that sperm when it tries to swim by— an IUD I'd come to loathe. AJ came with me that day, took a few hours off work for maybe half an hour of eventful pain. I lay on the table, legs spread like the doctor needed a wide-angle shot of my insides. AJ sat in a chair right beside my head. The doctor began to get everything ready:

So, I'm not going to numb it, so it WILL hurt, but I'll walk through everything as I'm doing it, okay?

I nodded.

What should I do? AJ asked.

I just barely turned my head to face him (I'm scared to move too much).

I took his hand, lacing our fingers together.

There was silence, then the ripping open of sterile instruments, a squirt of lubricant, and my doctor's gloved fingers spreading the curtains.

Breathe as I tell you; it'll help. Breathe in—

I clenched my teeth and breathed in through my nose.

She slid the speculum in and opened everything up. *Breathe out.*

She took a long brush sort of thing, but not the same one used for my pap smear.

Breathe in again—

I felt it touch the cervix, and my uterus clenched like my teeth. *And out.*

Now, I'm going to insert the IUD. It'll be bad cramping, but it should be only for a few moments. Take a big breath here when I push it in. I'll have to use some force.

I gripped AJ's hand tighter as I breathed in.

Hey, he says quietly. I glanced towards him. He was smiling at me, then sticking his tongue out, and then poking my nose with his tongue.

I do dingus things to help you feel better!

As his tongue touched my nose, the sudden pain arrived. It felt like my period cramps I'd gotten years ago, but this was higher than in my uterus, and it felt like there was an erupting volcano inside of me.

And then it was over.

Can combinations of pain, suffering, AND sex lead to bodily autonomy?

The American Psychological Association claims that "sixty-seven percent of heterosexual women admitted to occasionally faking orgasm," and that "most men don't believe it could happen to them, with only twenty percent saying they think their female partners might fake."[1]

For nearly the first year of our relationship, I lied to AJ. Well, not exactly; he'd just ask if I *finished* during sex, and I'd nod my head. Don't get me wrong, everything would feel *great*, but I just couldn't get there. The weird part is that I could *finish* just fine on my own, when I was in control. I did my best to tackle this issue with AJ early on in the relationship, actually. At the time, though, I just told him:

*It's hard for me to, ya know, *squelching noise* with you.*

Well, think about it; you've been with your body your whole life, and you know it really well—I don't know your body as well as you do, so it'll take time for both of us.

When I decided to finally tell him:

So, I, um, ya know, how I'll say that I finished after sexy time, well, I actually can't with you. I don't know why, but ever since we first talked about it months ago, how I was having trouble then, well, I still can't, and I feel awful for lying to you about it, and you can hate me, but I wanted to tell you, please, don't break up with me—

He snickered, chuckled even.

THAT'S what you were so worried about?

I nodded as tears formed their usual river down my cheeks.

He squeezed me.

That's fine, cute stuff. We can work on it together if you want to.

---

[1] Dingfelder, Sadie F. Understanding orgasm. (2011). *American Psychological Association*

"The men also reported they'd be distressed to find out their partners were faking."[2]

But AJ wasn't distressed one bit—the next time we had sex, before doing anything other than kiss me with his freckled lips, he asked me what he wanted me to do. He held his hand out to me, and I took it and set it right above my clit. I guided him through what to do, and he *listened*. He rubbed, stroked, and inserted as I told him to. The focus was on *me*, on *my body*. With some focus and determination, I could feel an orgasm creeping up inside of me. It built and built, then dissipated. But we continued, and I was determined to find it again. AJ thrust a dildo in and out as I kept the vibrator on my clit. Within another minute or two, *it* snuck up on me. I forced my eyes closed and suddenly sat up, my insides tensing up. He pulled the dildo out, got on top of me, gave me a kiss, and then it was *his* turn.

When I asked AJ for his input on me getting on birth control, his response was, *It's your body, so it's up to you.*

You can expect some blood and cramping for the first two to three months, but after that, it should stop, my doctor had told me after she'd forced that IUD into my cervix. I spent the rest of that day on my couch, a heating pad pressed against my uterus. I could barely move. Imagine normal period cramps or those uterus cramps you get at the most random times but amplified times ten. Everything hurt. I waited the two to three

---

[2] Ibid

months; I waited six months; I waited nine months; I couldn't wait any longer.

When I lay down to sleep at night.

When I rolled over in bed.

When I got up in the morning.

When I worked out *any* part of my body.

When I got turned on.

When AJ went in too deep and close to it.

When I laughed.

When I walked too much.

Whenever it wanted to.

These were only the most common times when the IUD caused me pain.

We can take it out if you want. You, by no means, have to ride it out if you don't think you can, my doctor reminded me every time I came in due to the pain.

I don't want to, not yet. I wanna see if it settles itself out.

My doctor became increasingly concerned once I told her the pain prevented me from going to the gym and being active. The semester before I got my double mastectomy done, I began to dedicate myself to the gym. My one wish after having this surgery was to develop a clean set of pecs on my chest. As I began to go to the gym four days a week, I could see them peeking out from underneath my breasts. After surgery, I eventually got back into my regular gym routine after some recovery. What felt like within weeks of pushing myself at the gym, there they were! I stared at my pecs in the bedroom mirror, the one I once wanted to cover entirely, and smiled.

However, for the entirety of the four or five months that that IUD was in me, I could not keep a regular gym schedule. I became a couch potato, and not in a nice, relaxing way. My mind and body begged for the gym, to do 30 minutes of cardio and some on the weight machines. My body started to slowly revert to being a tad chunkier, and my pecs threatened to disappear. One day, I thought I was in good enough shape to do a light gym day, but on the sit-up machine, my uterus screamed from inside me. I got off the machine and headed home, and I texted AJ: *I can't even do the smallest things at the gym anymore.*

I was baby-free, but I wasn't comfortable having
decent sex, couldn't go to the gym, could barely
walk some days—the list goes on.

When she finally *did* remove the IUD, I asked to speak to it. She held it in her hand, the white plastic *barely* ruined by being in this body for a handful of months. There were only small traces of blood on the device. But I couldn't say any words. *Maybe my body just didn't like you,* was all I could muster up in my thoughts. But boy, let me tell you, when she pulled it out, I felt a weight lifted off my uterus. The pain had already lessened, and it only continued until it was gone.

You've been with your body your whole life; you know it really well—

A conversation with my friend, Kelsey, after the IUD was removed due to ultimate failure:

I don't know what to do anymore,
that was my best option that wouldn't
interfere with the other hormones at all—

> *Well, is it the hormones that's concerning?*
> *I know there's a pill option with*
> *only one hormone in it*

There is? Maybe I can bring it up to
my doctor.

> *Yeah! (:*

It looks like it's even in the chart
she sent me in February explaining the different
birth control options ...

> *Maybe that one won't mess with the*
> *testosterone as much!*

My doctor told me this pill idea, the *mini pill* she called it, was a good idea. My IUD was the optimal choice because the goal of hormone replacement therapy is to boost levels of testosterone to induce a variation of "male puberty," and it would keep estrogen levels low so they don't counteract each other and stump progress. A normal IUD has both female sex hormones: estrogen and progesterone. *My* IUD had *just* progesterone, *and* it fed the hormone only to the uterus area, so the rest of the body would not have any adverse side effects from it. When we ended up having to remove it, I was stumped. This had been my *best* chance in my, my doctor's, and even my old endocrinologist's eyes. My doctor even consulted other, more experienced doctors to get their advice too, but the IUD said, *Fuck you,* and destroyed my uterus instead, to the point where I had to take painkillers *every day* to be able to even walk, something I hadn't had to take *that* often since high school.

By the time I was a senior in high school, my body had become immune to ibuprofen. It started in ninth-grade health class. We were learning about burns, and I was taking notes as the teacher flashed pictures on the screen of first-, second-, and third-degree burns. The skin was yellow, bubbly, even calloused. Once we got to the worst burns, my brain began to panic. Maybe the image was too gruesome for it to handle, I'm not sure, but once I saw that bubbly skin, all I saw was TV static. My body became warm, and my red basketball shorts stuck to my skin. I was slowly losing my vision. I focused on the cute guy sitting in front of me, Andrew, whom I had a crush on, but the static closed in on me. Within a minute, that was all I could see. I knew where the teacher was, so I raised my hand and asked to use the bathroom. She waved me along, and I stood up carefully, exited the classroom, and walked a couple of feet down the hall. My hands gripped the sides of the sink as I got my bearings. I turned the water on, splashed my face, and then I saw myself. I was *white.* I don't know how else to describe it; I just knew that it wasn't normal. But as I learned growing up, you don't go to the nurse unless you are throwing up or have a fever.

I returned to the classroom.

Since that day, at the most random times, I'd get that same sensation. It was never *quite* as extreme, but I learned the warning signs of when I would start to have what I realize now was probably some sort of panic attack. Since that day, I kept a water bottle with me at all times, just in case. The water helps bring me back. With these spells came physical symptoms of what would eventually be diagnosed as Generalized Anxiety Disorder (GAD). I felt sick *every morning,* like I had a small cold, my stomach became more and more unpredictable, to the point I couldn't eat before school, and I'd often feel light-headed. Once the cold-like symptoms, headaches, stuffy nose, etc., began, I took ibuprofen before school because mom said that's what you take when you feel sick. So, every day for the next three years, I took a dose of painkillers. All I knew was that it eased my symptoms, and I felt somewhat normal when I did.

If you take ibuprofen every day for *that* long, you risk digestion issues and stomach ulcers.

And after a while, the pills stopped helping. I had to take more and more to get the same effect, that *ease,* for my body. So, mom got me a Costco-sized bottle of naproxen sodium, what I call *super ibuprofen.* And lo and behold, it worked. To this day, ibuprofen has no effect on my body.

When my IUD was tearing apart my uterus, I stayed away from pain meds the best I could, and I *really* didn't want to rely on them like I once did. So, I got it removed. The question then was if this pill option would work, and there was only one way to find out. A week after that appointment, I took the first pill.

And it was *magical!* There wasn't any pain. I could go back to the gym, and I could stop taking naproxen. After a month, we tested my testosterone levels, and they hadn't changed, which meant that the pill was having no adverse effects. I was relieved. I was relieved that my body was finally at peace again. I'd destroyed it so much with the hormones, surgery, and then that IUD, but it was recuperating, settling down again. However, the testosterone would lead to another issue soon after I started these new pills.

I was watching a YouTube video where the YouTuber, who is also trans, was interviewing Buck Angel, a transsexual man who also used to be a porn star. The two of them discussed stuff that many people (even doctors) tend to ignore or just not tell patients going on testosterone nowadays: the negative side effects of the treatment, specifically that of vaginal atrophy.[3] This issue happens when your average woman goes through menopause, as the mucus lining of the vagina thins and becomes drier, leading to cramping, pain, bleeding, what have you. Normally, the lining is nice and plump and moist. However, if you take testosterone and don't supplement it with any estrogen, this problem occurs early, and in Buck Angel's case, it was bad enough that he nearly died.

The vagina stays wet, not just for sexual reasons—the wetness is what allows it to clean itself. The drier a vagina is, the less it can keep clean and the more prone to infections it is. But what controls how wet it can be? Estrogen. The vagina needs estrogen to stay wet and continuously clean. Testosterone is a *much* more powerful hormone than estrogen, so the levels dwindle when more of it is introduced. In Angel's case, his body was receiving testosterone but no estrogen. His estrogen levels were at zero. The vagina couldn't clean itself and developed an infection, which then became septic, or infected with large amounts of harmful bacteria. He had to be rushed to a hospital while vacationing in Mexico, and he was literally minutes from death. Many trans men want *no* estrogen in their bodies because it's a female hormone; however, if you have a vagina, you need the estrogen to go along with it.

---

[3] Trans Men's Vaginal Atrophy With Buck Angel. (2022). *YouTube*

Everyone, men and women, have estrogen in their bodies, just to varying degrees. When I watched this interview, I became worried. Sex had become a bit painful afterward, similar to the cramping coming from my IUD. Initially, it was my body getting used to the absence of the device, but by June (having the IUD removed in October of the prior year), this was no longer my body re-adjusting. I had a hunch, and my body told me to bring it up to my doctor. A week later, I did.

In June, I opened a rectangular box, similar in size to what a tube of toothpaste would come in, to a squeeze tube of *vaginal cream* and a plastic syringe. The directions on the side of the box were too vague for me to follow, so I ended up watching a YouTube video of someone using the instruments (I used the wrong side of the syringe the first time ... *why are the measurements at the bottom,* I asked myself). I watched the white cream push its way into the syringe before laying on the bathroom floor, spreading my legs, and carefully sliding the tube into myself (I now understand why guys have a hard time finding the hole). I pushed the stuff in, waited a moment, and then removed the tube. Then I went to bed. I have to do this right before bed so that way the vagina can absorb the estrogen overnight; if I'm up and moving, it'll just come back out.

After just one week of this ritual, done three nights a week, *everything* felt better. The cramping subsided for good this time, and at my check-up to see how progress was going, my doctor opened up the cave and peeked inside for not even ten seconds before saying, *That looks MUCH better than a few weeks ago; it's working!*

A week later, I emailed her:

> *Hi Dr. -------, I wanted to get your thoughts on this. There is still some small pain after I have sex with my boyfriend, not as bad as before, much less, but the same type of pain and area. We used lube once, and it helped, but I sometimes forget to use it. Is that really just the best solution?*

Her response:

> *Aarron, if you're having pain, I'd recommend using lube when you can. You might also consider switching positions and finding one that does not cause pain. You can also take pain medication afterward, or since the dosage of your cream is not so rigid, you can take more or less when needed. Maybe if you know you're going to see him at a certain time and will probably have sex, take some the night before as prep.*

I thought back to high school and taking those pills every morning. Since I'd been on *actual* anxiety medication, I'd limited how often I took naproxen. The pain was minimal, and I could live through it, but one day, I told myself *It's not all the time, just when you need it; plus, if you'd ever remember to use lube, you wouldn't need the pills*, and I took a dose. The pain subsided, and that was the only time I took them that week. *It's okay to take them when you need them*, I reminded myself.

So, I began to listen to my body. I upped my dosage of the cream just slightly and prioritized it in the days before I'd see AJ, just in case. When the pain came back, even just a little bit, I'd take just two pills to prevent it from hindering *anything*, and I even told AJ some more foreplay may be in order to get everything warmed up and ready to roll (I'm still working on the lube part). I *listened*, no, *respected* my body and what it needed. I was *able* to.

How I've respected my body (with myself and with others):

1. Paid talented artists hundreds of dollars to force art into my skin

2. Got a flattering haircut the week before my boy-friend's older brother's wedding

3. Shaved my face when the stubble got too unruly

4. Went to my doctor for OBGYN issues once I began to have regular sex

5. Had regular sex

6. Paid a kind doctor in Washington, D.C., to remove my breasts via a bilateral double mastectomy

Respecting and *loving* a body is a lot more work
than I initially thought.

The side effects of the birth control were:

Nausea, vomiting, headache, bloating, breast tenderness, or weight gain may occur. Vaginal bleeding between pe-riods (spotting) or missed/irregular periods may occur. If any of these effects last or get worse, tell your doctor or pharmacist promptly. If you miss 2 periods in a row (or 1 period if the pill has not been used properly), contact your doctor for a pregnancy test. Remember that this medication has been prescribed because your doctor has judged that the benefit to you is greater than the risk of side effects. Many people using this medication do not have serious side effects. This medication may raise your blood pressure. Check your blood pressure regularly and tell your doctor if the results are high. Tell your doctor right away if you have any serious side effects, including: lumps in the breast, mental/mood changes (such as new/worsening depression), severe stomach/abdominal pain, unusual changes in vaginal bleeding (such as continuous spotting, sudden heavy bleeding, missed periods), dark urine, yellowing eyes/skin. This medication may rarely cause serious (sometimes fatal) problems from blood clots (such as deep vein thrombosis, heart attack, pulmonary embolism, stroke). Get medical help right away if any of these side effects occur: chest/jaw/left arm pain, confusion, sudden dizziness/fainting, pain/swelling/warmth in the groin/calf, trouble speaking, sudden shortness of breath/rapid breathing, unusual headaches (including headaches with vision changes/lack of coordination, worsening of migraines, sudden/very severe headaches), unusual sweating, weakness on one side of the body, vision problems/changes (such as double vision, partial/complete blindness). A very serious allergic reaction to this drug is rare. However, get medical help right away if you notice any symptoms of a serious allergic reaction, including: rash, itching/swelling (especially of the face/tongue/throat), severe dizziness, trouble breathing.

At the very end of this exhaustive list, it said, *This is not a complete list of possible side effects.*

The way I described my desires to my surgeon that day—*I want to see my real self. I want to make this body mine*—sometimes I feel I've achieved that, and other times I don't.

I was still sore the morning after I lost my virginity to Cody. There was no comfort in this sexual pain, no hugs, reassurance, just *sore*. At night, often 2 a.m. once AJ and I finally get to sleep, if my uterus is hurting because we had sex, he pulls me close to his fuzzy, warm chest. My back touches his chest hair, and it's comforting. His hands wrap around me, and he does something I taught him to do back when the IUD would daily cause much more intense pain—he sets his hands over my uterus, right over the top of the pubic mound, and presses just a little. He holds his hands there for a few minutes, keeping the pressure steady. I eventually fall asleep once the pain has subsided because of his hands.

Our sex might emit pain if we're not careful, but his body can remove it even more easily.

The frog must change over and over every time a predator threatens it. I, too, must change when my own self threatens me. I told myself that my third-grade squish was ugly—I told myself I was a boy—I told myself I was unlovable in this body unless I gave myself a penis—I told myself so many things; I was confronted so many times by my own predator.
Myself.
So, I changed.

YES,
THIS BODY IS MINE

AJ held himself up on all fours above me. Our lips mingled as he slid his shorts and underwear off, then my own. He rubbed his body against mine, reaching a hand down and squeezing my ass. He positioned his hips lower, thrusting them just barely to signal that he wanted in. He squeezed my skin tighter as he made his way in, but once he reached halfway, I pulled my lips away from his, asking if he could *prepare her* a bit more before he started to rearrange my insides. He pulled out and looked down at himself:

It doesn't look to me like she needs to be prepared more.

Please, just a little more?

I thought back to what the doctor had told me: to use lubrication, do more foreplay, and take pain medication if I need to. He took a few more minutes to work magic down below before resuming his place above me, putting himself inside all the way this time.

I see a body—
that has no scar to stare at every time it puts socks on;
that doesn't have a distorted pointer;
with knees the correct color;
with clean wrists;
unscarred by a tether ball game;
with narrowed hips and a flatter ass;

with the smallest tummy possible;
with nipples I can feel;
that is flat without needing to cut;
with more hair and less of a forehead;
that can create life;
that can have sex wherever, whenever, without jumping through hoops.

I see a body that cannot exist.

The frog changes itself from what is expected to something surprising. It distorts, mutilates even, its body for protection. I am that frog. My body had to change for it to become one that I could live in. My body has to be *mine* to survive. I wonder if *that's* why I'd hack into my wrists at least once a day throughout high school, to show my eyes that this body is mine. Does that scar on my foot make my body mine? Does my chest make my body mine? What about the tattoos?

The first thing that stood out to me when I met AJ was that his hair and beard color were different. His hair is more of a light brown color, while his beard is nearly all red, with some blonde thrown in at the roots. I can also tell you that he has a multitude of tattoos, ranging from a half-realistic, half-geometric monkey to some cool gear patterns. He has pale blue eyes that shine in the sunlight, and his lip freckles are gifts from God. AJ's body is a *mixture*—parts of him came naturally, things that make him who he is; other parts were added.

But it's all *him*.

Stephen, the guy who I hooked up with at the abandoned asylum, had an ice cream tattoo. Q had cow paintings in his room. Mike had dreadlocks. I barely remember, nor do I care for any of these men anymore, but I can still think of what made them *them* (in *my* mind, at least).

I asked AJ what makes my body *mine* through his eyes: *Your hair. You're always worried about your hair. We'll be getting ready to go somewhere, and you'll be like, "Wait, I gotta do my hair; it's a mess." He* continued: *I also think of your butt when I think of you. Like, have you seen that thing? Dang, now THAT'S a booty!*

I see a body—
that *has* a white scar to stare at every time I put socks on;
that *has* a distorted pointer;
with *differently-colored* knees;
with *marked* wrists;
scarred by a tether ball game;
with *wider-than-normal* hips and a *big ass*;
with an *anatomically correct* tummy;
with nipples I *cannot* feel;
a chest that is flat *by* needing to cut;
with *less* hair and *more* of a forehead;
that *wants* to create life;
that *cannot* have sex wherever, whenever, without jumping through hoops.

I see a body that is real, that is mine.

Maybe I don't need to achieve *bodily autonomy, confidence, pride.*
Maybe I've already found it without realizing it.

But still—when my dad came to me before I had my chest surgery those years ago, I was sitting at the kitchen table, minding my own business, when I heard his footsteps approaching from behind. He knelt beside me as if talking to a five-year-old. He looked up at me: *You know, you're really upsetting your mother with all this. Why would you mutilate your body?*

When I stood in front of that mirror, in front of the collage
of yellows, purples, and oranges—
maybe my mutilation did NOT make me pretty.

However—when I lay shirtless in AJ's lap and he ran his fingers across my scars; when I lay beside him in bed and he put an arm around me to hold me close; when I told him, *I haven't shaved down there in a week, sorry,* yet his mouth still enjoyed itself; when my IUD destroyed our sex life and his fingers came out caked in blood; when I stood naked in the hotel bathroom getting the shower warmed up, and he wandered in and fucked me on the four-star sink; when he marked *Jizz in Aarron day* in his phone calendar two weeks after my IUD is inserted; when he told me, *It's your body, so it's your choice,* when I asked him for his input on birth control methods, that he'd be fine with using condoms all the time; when he introduced me to his older brother, then sister and her partner, and finally his mother; when I couldn't have sex for two weeks *before* my IUD was put in, but after a long weekend trip to Iowa, we had it anyways, and he told me that he missed fucking me; when he told me I'm cute the first day we started talking on Grindr; when—

Although I may have a harder time believing AJ when he says that he doesn't mind my lack of breasts, my excess fat on my tummy, my thinning hair, and my problematic and often angry vagina, I still believe him when he tells me that he loves my thighs.

I feel like that since you tell me that you love me every day, I'm starting to believe it more and more, I tell AJ.

AND I WILL LOVE THIS BODY HOWEVER NECESSARY

When I sat in my old endocrinologist's office, listening about all the side effects of testosterone. *A deeper voice, body hair, genital growth, possible infertility,* she told me. I didn't mind the idea of infertility then: *I never want to have biological kids,* I told her. But my mom still asked, *Are you sure?* I began to inject myself in my stomach, inner thighs, and outer thighs every week for the rest of my life.

But then I sent a text to my best friend:

> *I feel like I'd have a child with AJ. For my whole life*
> *I've only wanted to adopt, but I feel like*
> *I'd be okay with having a baby with him ...*
> *I've never had that feeling before*

I told AJ that I didn't want to *carry* a child, that we should look into a surrogate. I Googled the cost for one, and the average minimum is $30,000. The average cost of having a baby yourself is less than half that at around $13,000. With decent insurance, the cost can even be as low as $500. I've always been a money-conscious person, so carrying a single kid myself sounds like the better option in that sense.

But can I mentally handle carrying a baby?

A study was done on pregnancy and transgender men; "twenty-five (61%) transgender men reported using testosterone before pregnancy ... Among those who had used testosterone, twenty (80%) reported resuming menstruation within 6 months after stopping testosterone. Five participants (20%) conceived while still amenorrheic from testosterone use. After pregnancy, six (38%) participants who had not previously used testosterone before pregnancy initiated use. Ten participants (40%) who had previously been on testosterone reported that they had not yet resumed testosterone use after pregnancy."[1]

There's a possibility ...

"Two-thirds of pregnancies were planned," with "most transgender men [becoming] pregnant within four months of trying."[2]

That if I really wanted to ...

"A higher proportion of transgender men who had used testosterone underwent cesarean delivery compared with those

---

[1] Light, Alexis D. MD, MPH; Obedin-Maliver, Juno MD, MPH; Sevelius, Jae M. PhD; Kerns, Jennifer L. MD, MPH. Transgender Men Who Experienced Pregnancy After Female-to-Male Gender Transitioning. Obstetrics & Gynecology: December 2014 - Volume 124 - Issue 6 - p 1120-1127

[2] Ibid

who reported no testosterone use (36% compared with 19%, respectively)."[3]

I could have a baby with this man I love, who taught me that I could be loved. That I deserve love.

We stand in line for a concert in the drizzle. My teal cat-and-dog umbrella keeps us dry except for our calves and the backs of our ankles. We got there an hour before the doors opened so we could get inside and find a decent spot. This space feels oddly personal, even though people are in front of and behind us, but they're in their own little worlds, too. Every couple and group are talking with themselves. AJ and I discuss how adorable it would be to bring our future child, who we have nicknamed Little HAP, per her assumed initials, to concerts, complete with oversized metal T-shirts and noise-canceling headphones. We continue to talk about kids and discuss surrogacy in our future, but I tell him it is expensive. He asks me, "Well, can *you* not carry a baby?" I tell him no, and he asks why. I remind him that biological men do not carry babies, and if I want to be as close to a biological man as possible, I shouldn't either.

Having a baby is a woman's thing.

Or maybe having a baby is a *female* thing, and my body is and always will be *female.*

[3.] Ibid

"Egg quality and quantity were similar between transgender men and women ... While taking testosterone, ovulation may stop (usually within 6 to 12 months), but egg reserves don't disappear."[4]

One day, after I take a shower, I stand in front of the bathroom mirror. I turn to the side and lean my torso back a bit so that my stomach sticks out a bit more. I set a hand on my stomach, making it look rounder. I am silent, just staring. I think about the first time I went to therapy to figure out what was going on regarding my sex and gender mismatch between my mind and body—my therapist, Cathy, asked me if I'd ever felt any maternal instinct, *felt like a woman*, she phrased it. *No, I told her.*

---

4. Arquilla, Emelia DO. Transgender Pregnancy: Moving Past Misconceptions. (2020). *Healthline*

WHAT IS A MAN?

I take to the internet to do as much research as I can: *Transgender men being pregnant, bodily changes during pregnancy, transgender pregnancy, costs of pregnancy.* I look at photos of pregnant transgender men.

My brain and body are confused.

These men look normal but other-worldly at the same time. Their backs are arched forward like mine was in front of the mirror, their uteruses filled with life, their chests still flat, though. *Are these men?* I ask myself. My body tells me they are: *They're just making use of what their bodies can do; you should, too.* My brain tells me that they aren't: *They've gone back on all the effort they put into transitioning. Men don't get pregnant.*

A participant in the study on pregnancy stated that "pregnancy and childbirth were very male experiences for me. When I birthed my children, I was born into fatherhood."[1]

---

[1] Light, Alexis D. MD, MPH; Obedin-Maliver, Juno MD, MPH; Sevelius, Jae M. PhD; Kerns, Jennifer L. MD, MPH. Transgender Men Who Experienced Pregnancy After Female-to-Male Gender Transitioning. Obstetrics & Gynecology: December 2014 - Volume 124 - Issue 6 - p 1120-1127

I can imagine the moment we create life within me—he holds my body close to his, my face pressed against the side of his neck (the skin is so gentle and soft). I breathe against his skin in sync with his thrusts, his own inhalations becoming quicker. Maybe I pull my head back from his skin, place a hand on his cheek, and give him a long, love-filled kiss as I feel his body throb within my own.

But can I handle another drastic change to my body? One that would seemingly bring me further from my goal of being a normal man?

It's nearly the ten-year anniversary of when I made that first wound on my wrist with my lead pencil in the middle of math class. I poked a little lead through the hole and ran it down my skin, watching the light line it made both from the lead itself drawing on the peach-colored skin and from the gentle breaking of that skin. I went back up the skin, making another lead line and more of a dent. After that moment, something in my being could sense there was no going back. Mutilation, whether done with 0.7-sized lead or a surgeon's scalpel, is not something one can come back from. *Birthing a child* is not something one can come back from.

The female body has to change in order to carry out birth, changes that take over nine months to complete, and so afterward, it has to get itself back to normal, or as *normal* as it can be after the traumatic event.

The first week after delivery, the vagina will bleed heavily right after birth, but it will lighten up over time and as the uterus reverts back to its normal size. As the excess hormones leave the body, women's mental health typically declines, and the "high" of giving birth wears off.

In the second week, bleeding will continue to slowly taper off. This time frame is also typically when post-partum depression sets in.

By week six, bleeding typically stops, as the uterus is back to normal size.

Most pain and issues are resolved within six months.

One year after the little potato is welcomed into the world, "you may be feeling back to yourself, but your body may still feel slightly different—whether it's a few extra pounds, or just weight distributed in different places."[2]

When I had my double mastectomy, I held onto the fact that my body would get back to normal eventually, even when I saw those colors and wounds in the mirror, when the seroma obscured my chest. If I were to house a child within my body, everything would go back to normal eventually, too, but what if my body doesn't *quite* go back to normal?

But there is one key difference between the time when
I had my double mastectomy and in the future if I were to
carry a child—

I'd have AJ by my side the whole journey, a man who loves me and my body for what we are and a man who taught *me* to love myself and my body for what we are.

---

[2] Ernst, Holly PA-C. Your Guide to Postpartum Recovery. (2018). *Healthline*

Does creating, carrying, and birthing a child count as mutilation, too?

Maybe I want to mutilate my body just one more time with a fetus like I have with the toothpicks, the tattoos, the piercings, the surgery, the hormones, the cream I have to stick up my vagina *because* of the hormones.

But is mutilation always a bad thing?

Is it *mutilation*, or is it *chosen pain*?

A few months after I met AJ, and we started dating, I *knew* he had come into my life for a reason. It felt so *perfect*, so *natural*, like there was no way it could just be a coincidence. I think about all the aspects of my life that brought me to where I am—I think about the fact that if I had gained *bodily autonomy* how I wanted years ago, I wouldn't have him with me, excited to one day buy a house and start a family. The most common narrative for transgender people is that we're born in the wrong body, and maybe some people feel that way, but if I hadn't been born in *this* body, would I have ever learned to love it?

If I do decide to house our own child one day, will I still love my body?

Can I?

Two primary themes associated with transgender men and pregnancy were isolation and gender dysphoria. Pregnant men do not exist in my mind; this is not something my fiancé or my brother could achieve. As one participant puts it, "We exist. And we are different."[3] Participants were torn when discussing gender dysphoria around pregnancy—some felt more connected to their bodies, using them for what they were designed to do, and others felt a new dissonance. *Men don't get pregnant.*

When I was little—my mom and I sat in the minivan while at a stoplight. Every day when I would come home, *Oprah* would be on the TV, and later, when I was in high school, it would be *The Ellen Show*, and in 2008, all the mid-day talk shows were talking about one single person: Thomas Beatie, "the pregnant man." While we were stopped at that light, I turned to my mom to question her about what was up with that man on TV—

How did that man on TV get pregnant? Men can't get pregnant ...
Well, he has female parts instead of male parts.
How did he get them?
He was born that way.
But HOW?

I don't think my child mind could quite comprehend how a person who was a *man* could create and birth a child just like a *woman* normally would. But when my mom explained this to me, her tone made it sound normal, like it was just a thing that happened. Although I couldn't understand how this man

---

3. Light, Alexis D. MD, MPH; Obedin-Maliver, Juno MD, MPH; Sevelius, Jae M. PhD; Kerns, Jennifer L. MD, MPH. Transgender Men Who Experienced Pregnancy After Female-to-Male Gender Transitioning. Obstetrics & Gynecology: December 2014 - Volume 124 - Issue 6 - p 1120-1127

had what I had and did *female things*, I could understand that it was just a thing that exists, just a type of person who exists.

My current self has no more confusion—maybe this man, too, grew up hating his body, being instructed that it was to be hidden, that young boys would lust over it if it was revealed; maybe his mom also instructed him on the importance of shaving as a girl, the necessity of it; maybe he also shoved bouncy balls down his pants in middle school, feeling embarrassed by the urge; maybe he too removed his breasts out of revulsion; maybe he too thought about his breasts years after they were removed; maybe he was once disgusted by the idea of sex until it was all he could turn to in order to feel valued; maybe he sat on strangers' dicks to become *something*, even if that something is *just a body*; he must have become more than *just a body*, maybe he also found his AJ; maybe he got back his *bodily autonomy*, and maybe that's how he was able to be "the pregnant man" back in 2008.

The Butterfly Effect is the idea, developed by Edward Lorenz, that "some complex dynamical systems exhibit unpredictable behaviors such that small variances in the initial conditions could have profound and widely divergent effects on the system's outcomes."[4]

In other words, even the smallest change
to my existence, my past, could have changed
where I ended up, where my *body* ended up.

---

[4] Vernon, Jamie L., Understanding the Butterfly Effect. (2017). *American Scientist*, (105)3, 130.

How my *love* for this body ended up.

But what does this mean for all the things I've put my body through? If I want to have a child, should I have kept my breasts to feed them? Should I have just not gone through the trauma and pain of my IUD if I ended up wanting to have a child anyway? Could the testosterone I have been taking for five years have messed with my fertility?

I can imagine it: AJ and I sitting in the doctor's office, my skin crinkling the paper gown. The fertility specialist had just asked me question after question: How long have you been taking testosterone? And when was the last time you got your period? And now we sit. Maybe he holds my hand; maybe I don't want to be touched. We wait for her to come back, to tell us if it was successful or not—if I could still produce a biological child or if I'd ruined my chances.

When the IUD didn't work and my doctor and I were discussing the mini pill, I asked her what to do until I started the new pill; her response was, *I'm honestly not too worried; with your medical history, I don't think you're very fertile at all.*

Texts between AJ and I:

> So, say we decide one day to create
> our own small child

Would you be bummed out if it
didn't work bc of me?

No

But what if one day we want a
baby and cannot make one?

I'll still love you
We can look at a surrogate

I just need to accept what my body has become—

And proceed with life given the cards I was dealt.

A JOURNEY CONTINUES

If I hadn't found AJ and allowed him to help me love my body. If I hadn't lost my virginity when and how I did. If I hadn't learned to hate sex and then learned to love it. If I hadn't had my double mastectomy and experienced the immediate regret after seeing what I'd gotten myself into. If I hadn't used and thrown out all the house's bouncy balls. If I hadn't named my *squish* that day while sitting on the carpet—

Once again, I find Melissa Febos and myself somewhat similar—"most forms of healing include hurt, and many include violence ... and chosen pain should not be mistaken for self-hatred."[1]

Chosen pain. A baby. If I have a baby, it will be painful mentally, emotionally, and physically. Maybe just one more bout of chosen pain. I feel comfortable in this body, finally—I can take it. I choose this pain one more time.

AJ sent me a picture he took right before his older brother's wedding. I saw my hair, thin but still resting tastefully on my head, quaffed just how I like it; my shirt that didn't even fit me

---

[1] Febos, Melissa. The feminist case for breast reduction. (May 11, 2022). *NYTimes*

anymore after I'd gained some more muscle at the gym (I had my IUD in at the time of the picture, so I wasn't as muscle-y since I couldn't go to the gym); the tie AJ loaned me that looks too long for my body (it's even longer than my torso); fitting black dress pants that hugged my hips and thighs, hips and thighs that come out too far and are too big; a smile on my face, one that is genuine—I've always loved dressing in fancy clothes. He'd shown me this picture before, and every time, my eyes darted to my hips. They're too wide, and my pants are too fitting. I never saved the picture when he'd send it to me, telling me, *Look how cute you are! [heart eyes emoji]*. But this time, I saved it. I even made it my profile picture on Twitter.

I do not like the hips, but still, kinda cute.

EPILOGUE

134

There are certain aspects of my body I can change about myself—my weight, my hair, my breasts, the period, my voice—but with these changes, the self-loathing remains, along with the self-love. Now, it tells me to have a baby—something I have tried to protect myself against since I was young. I even went on hormones under the assumption I'd never want to conceive with this body, this body that strives so much to be seen as a man's. I need to change my body now, too, but not in ways I'd expected. I stopped taking my hormones and started taking daily folic acid. My body began to bleed only a month later. My body will bleed again every month until it gets what it desires—a baby. My body embraces this pain to prepare for a child. I plan to change my body again, but this time to create new life. I will choose this pain if it means I can find the joy of having a family with this man I love.

ACKNOWLEDGMENTS

I have so many people to thank. Seeing this project in print is still hard for me to believe, but the team at Atmosphere Press believed in *The Body of a Frog* and gave it the care it deserved. Thank you to the entire Atmosphere Press team, especially Tammy Letherer, my editor, who worked to turn this manuscript into the memoir she knew it could be. Thank you also to Dr. Rachael Hanel of Minnesota State University, Mankato, who saw this manuscript first and helped me get it off the ground. Thank you also to my creative writing peers at my graduate and undergraduate institutions, whose feedback and input have allowed my writing to truly blossom into art. Dr. Christine Spillson and Dr. John Nieves of Salisbury University were the first creative writing professors to tell me that I was an essayist, and I'm happy to tell them both that now I'm a memoirist, too. Thank you especially to my fiancé AJ, who taught me that I'm worthy of love regardless of my past. I can't wait to spend the rest of my life with you. Endless thank yous to my parents, family, and friends, who are always excited to hear about and are supportive of my writing endeavors. Finally, thank you to Maggie Nelson, Barrie Jean Borich, and Alison Bechdel, whose own books inspired my own. Excerpts and variations of this memoir have appeared in *Polaris*, *The Broadkill Review*, *The McNeese Review*, *O:JA&L*, and *WORDPEACE*.

ABOUT ATMOSPHERE PRESS

Founded in 2015, Atmosphere Press was built on the principles of Honesty, Transparency, Professionalism, Kindness, and Making Your Book Awesome. As an ethical and author-friendly hybrid press, we stay true to that founding mission today.

If you're a reader, enter our giveaway for a free book here:

SCAN TO ENTER
BOOK GIVEAWAY

If you're a writer, submit your manuscript for consideration here:

SCAN TO SUBMIT
MANUSCRIPT

And always feel free to visit Atmosphere Press and our authors online at atmospherepress.com. See you there soon!

ABOUT THE AUTHOR

AARRON SHOLAR is a transgender writer and author whose essays have been nominated for The Pushcart Prize and Best of the Net. He holds an MFA from MSU, Mankato and a BA from Salisbury University. He serves as the Prose Editor for Beaver Magazine and is starting his career as a Technical Writer and Editor in the corporate world. You can interact with him on Twitter/X @aarron_sholar.